86-1473

PN4193   McManus, Ed
.R63   We're roasting Harry
M38   Tuesday night

WE'RE ROASTING HARRY TUESDAY NIGHT . . .

How to Plan, Write, and Conduct the Business/Social Roast

WE'RE ROASTING HARRY TUESDAY NIGHT. . .

How to Plan, Write, and Conduct the Business/Social Roast

Ed McManus and Bill Nicholas

Prentice-Hall, Inc.
Englewood Cliffs, New Jersey

Prentice-Hall International, Inc., *London*
Prentice-Hall of Australia, Pty. Ltd., *Sydney*
Prentice-Hall Cananda Inc., *Toronto*
Prentice-Hall of India Private Ltd., *New Delhi*
Prentice-Hall of Japan, Inc., *Tokyo*
Prentice-Hall of Southeast Asia Pte. Ltd., *Singapore*
Whitehall Books, Ltd., *Wellington, New Zealand*
Editora Prentice-Hall do Brasil, Ltda., *Rio de Janeiro*

©1984 by
Prentice-Hall, Inc.
Englewood Cliffs, N.J.

Library of Congress Cataloging in Publication Data
McManus, Ed
    We're roasting Harry Tuesday night—.
    Includes index.
    1. Roasts (Public speaking) I. Nicholas, Bill,
        II. Title.
PN4193.R63M38 1984   808.5′1   83-24690

ISBN 0-13-950163-0

ISBN 0-13-950155-X {PBK}

Printed in the United States of America

With many thanks and appreciation to Judy, Kay, our families, the National Association of Spotlighters Inc. (a.k.a. "the Spotlighters") with particular nods to Flo Di Giacomo and Bill McDonald, the Friars Club, and jokesmiths extraordinaires Ray Fortune, Frank Keaney, and Arthur S. Dandeneau.

A Word from the Authors About Roasts

We bid you welcome to the Business/Social Roast.

In the pages of our book you will find a collection of ideas and experiences assembled by the authors over a collective five decades of planning, writing, and conducting Roasts for business, political, theatrical, educational, and religious groups and personalities. One of the earliest messages we want to bring to you is that the Roast is intended to be, and always should be, good-humored fun. We accomplish this through the tongue-in-cheek public recognition of our honored guest's human foibles which are often real, frequently imagined, and always exaggerated. Our Roast, properly conducted and governed by the interlocking parameters of good judgment and good taste, is as appropriate in the parish hall as it is in the smoking parlor.

Ed McManus, the business half of our writing team, has been involved in planning, writing, and conducting business Roasts over the past twenty years for a variety of large and small firms. Ed's forte is the considered approach with the relevant and penetrating one-liner based on a sure knowledge of the subject, the occasion, and the Roast craft.

Bill Nicholas, the theatrical half of our team, has been a successful comic, master of ceremonies, and Roast Master in his own right for close to thirty years. Bill brings to the book the sort of comedic knowledge and story-gathering and telling ability which can only come from having earned a living on stage facing a large, and not always too friendly, audience. (Bill says they were always friendly when he started.)

Together, the authors will share with you their ideas and experiences as to when to use the Roast vehicle versus some other form of recognition, and, once that decision has been made, how to begin the planning process.

You will learn about the need to interview the guest of honor long before any concrete Roast plans are formed and how to complete the all-important Roast Profile Worksheet (which we consider one of the most significant parts of the book).

You will learn how to find, collect, write and rewrite jokes that are both funny and relevant, and then how to blend them into a unified and smooth-flowing comedic monologue which can be presented by any average personality willing to invest the rehearsal time; one who can stand in front of a live microphone and not freeze or (even worse than that) try to monopolize the whole evening.

You will hear a good deal more about the Master of Ceremonies, or Roast Master, and the key role this person plays in the conduct of the successful Roast.

Finally we'll discuss the conduct of the Roast itself and share some anecdotes along the way. You'll learn why Roast Masters carry three-pronged adaptor plugs and extension cords with them, and why you shouldn't be surprised when the waiters drop all the silverware on the nearby kitchen floor during the most important part of someone's speech.

At the very end of the book, you'll see what a Roast segment should look like as it is sketched by an actual Roast Profile Worksheet and filled in from our own personal collection of Best Roast Lines. In this latter section, our second most proud accomplishment, you will find crisp, timely, relevant material which you can either use as is or, with modest effort, rewrite along the lines we will show you to bring a sense of understanding of your subject (as well as a sense of humor) to the Roast event. We will encourage you to believe that there is no such thing as a new joke. There are only new treatments of old jokes. What was funny about the Roman Centurion who painted one side of his sports chariot silver and the other side gold (in order to confuse the witnesses) is probably still funny about the young Navy Lieutenant who paints his Corvette the same way. The only difference you will see is that the latter is freshened, brought up to date, and used in a setting more readily accepted by your Roast audience.

We will ask you to remember, whatever else you have heard or read, that nothing is more important to the successful Roast than timely, topical, relevant, funny material properly selected and suited to the Guest of Honor, the occasion, and the audience.

Here is an illustrative anecdote:

We have been discussing the need and market for a book of this type for the past few years without doing much about making it happen. Finally, several months ago, we agreed to conduct an informal search program and learn exactly how many books have been written on the subject of planning, conducting, and writing the Roast. We looked independently and we looked thoroughly. We found none.

There were joke books to be sure, some very good and some very bad. We read hundreds of them. There were collections and anthologies and confederations of insults, one-liners, anecdotes, puns, witticisms, peppy retorts, and funny stories of nearly every stripe, but nothing that we could find on how to bring it all together. We decided to call the Friar's Club in New York and get the final word on how the Roast is done.

The Friar's Club, as you may know, is a fraternal group of show business people who enjoy each other's company and do a lot of charitable work along their merry road to having a good time—the best of both worlds. Anyway, we figured if this loosely knit theatrical clan didn't actually invent the Roast in the early days of this century, they at least played a major role in bringing it to the public's attention through their televised Roasts of such theatrical personalities as Jack Benny, Bob Hope, Ed Sullivan, and Johnny Carson, which have become classics of the genre.

Taking the direct approach, we telephoned their New York headquarters and asked to speak with the "Friar" in charge of their Roast activities. After a slight pause, a gentleman came on the line and asked the nature of our inquiry. He listened politely while we explained that we were Roast Masters ourselves and were coming to the source to learn first hand how it was done by the masters. He seemed pleased with this, and told us that there was no manual or policy book per se on the subject. There was a body of custom and tradition which had grown up and been preserved over the several decades that the Friars have been conducting Roasts, officially beginning with the Milton Berle fund-raising Roast in 1949.

"I can tell you, however, what we have found to be the three most important ingredients of the successful Roast," he said. We begged for the secret.

"The three most important ingredients are," he concluded, "Writers, Writers, and Writers."

Ed McManus
Bill Nicholas

Contents

WE'RE ROASTING HARRY TUESDAY NIGHT . . .

How to Plan, Write, and Conduct the Business/Social Roast

1

The Successful Roast . . . A Dash of History, Definitions and Ingredients

We don't know exactly when the Roast began as a free-standing social event but it goes back, no doubt, to unrecorded antiquity; back to the after-dinner speeches held around warrior campfires in the very earliest days of human history. While the day's hunt cooked, sparks jumped, and the smoke curled, the warriors would boast in word and song about their bravery and accomplishments and receive the thanks of their peers for the meal to be eaten and the anticipation of the next meal yet to come on another day.

Socrates, of course, was an after-dinner speaker, as was the blind poet, Homer. His tales of heroism and the soaring greatness of the human spirit are as alive today as they were when he sang them to his Greek audiences nearly three thousand years ago.

We know that in ancient Sicily, somewhere around 500 B.C., an orator named Corax opened a school on public and after-dinner speaking, and taught his craft to the politicians and other would-be speechmakers of his day. He even wrote a book on the subject, and, were it not out of print, it might be found remarkably similar to such books on the market today.

By the middle ages, or middle modern times, the dinner had come to be regarded as the one time during the day when the extended family of each noble estate could come together. It was a time for feasting and for expressing thanks to the Good Lord and to the Master of the Estate (not necessarily in that order) for the bountiful table which the people had placed before them. It was during this period that the jester made his debut, and soon, among the tales of bravery and great deeds, the acrobats and jugglers, there was a touch of coarse humor provided by the little man in the bells and scalloped cape who, for his counselor, did ". . .lead an ape." (Henry Wadsworth Longfellow, *Tales of a Wayside Inn*, "The Sicilian's Tale.")

Editor's Note: A jester could be punished both for not being funny enough or for being too funny at a time when the Master preferred a more solemn mood. Being a jester was a tough and thankless job. Also, it was still far too early for such one-liners as: "Take my wife, please!" Noblemen of the day could be very literal!

Moving rapidly to more recent times, we find many of the age-old traditions continued and expanded upon. The after-dinner speech was still used to communicate news of great deeds and to bring the extended family together on some common theme, but now we find more emphasis on an attempt to influence the listeners to some particular religious or political course of action and also, occasionally, to entertain.

By the middle of the last century, the after-dinner speech was a firmly entrenched tradition in the modern Western world. It was used to entertain, inform, and persuade, with political figures especially using the forum to express their views and to seek support for themselves, their candidates, or for whatever political objective absorbed them at the moment.

It is not exactly clear when the after-dinner speech made the transition into the Roast as we know it today. It is fair to assume that Mark Twain and his contemporaries had a great deal to do with it. In fact, by the early decades of this century, the Roast was fairly common in theatrical circles and organizations like the Masquers and the Friars were playing a major role in the evolution of the Roast into its present format.

Since a large part of the Roast's entertainment value comes from the humor and good fellowship which inevitably spring from a group of congenial people sharing good food, and perhaps even good wine, the one-liners and incisive comments came into being naturally as a good way to both get a laugh and make a point.

Before we leave the nineteenth century entirely, I would like to share one of these classic lines with you:

General U. S. Grant had left the Civil War battle lines for Washington where he was required by the President to address a group of influential and politically important lawyers. They had concluded dinner and were sitting around the stove for cognac and cigars, when one of them remarked to Grant that he looked like he had been through hell. "I have," he replied. "What was it like?" they eagerly asked. "Same as here," answered the General, "lawyers closest to the fire."

With the passing years and changing attitudes, the Roast has gone from a theatrical "in" joke to essentially worldwide acceptance anywhere free people can laugh, joke, speak their minds without fear, and not stumble too badly over the ironic premise that a guest can be honored through the recognition, exaggeration, and public announcement of all his faults, real or imagined. We just naturally assume that our Harry would rather be recognized through this controlled hostility than not be recognized at all.

So, we say with comic Joey Adams (perhaps the #1 Roast Master of them all): "If you can't say anything nice . . . let's hear it!"

THE ROAST DEFINED

What is a Roast anyway?

Let's consider Webster's definition of ". . .cooking over an open fire or in hot ashes. . ." This definition, while never intended to cover the sort of social/business Roast we have in mind, does at least communicate the proper message that our guest of honor could be in just a little bit of trouble. Not enough trouble to be fatal, certainly, or even to inflict permanent scars; but a splendid enough sufficiency that he can feel the heat warming his backside and wonder, with Shakespeare, how many of the words being allegedly spoken in jest really carry the speaker's own version of truth and reality.

We consider the Roast to be a positive recognition vehicle in which the honored guest's person, accomplishments, foibles and eccentricities are exaggerated for comic effect through jokes and anecdotes which are neither harmful nor necessarily true, but often funny.

Comic effect, humor, jokes and the like are all relative terms. What is humor? What is a joke? The serious student of humor might tell you that there are just six basic jokes. They really mean six basic joke categories and they are probably right. You must remember that with just ten Arabic characters (1 through 9 plus 0) we can make an almost infinite combination of numbers. So too, within our six basic joke categories we can construct an almost limitless number of treatments and versions of a basic comedic thought.

Let's briefly review these six joke categories:

THE JOKE OF SYMPATHY OR IDENTIFICATION

The thought behind this joke seems to be "that could have been me" or "that is the sort of thing I would have done." Here we find some common human foible played for comedic effect.

Example: Harry's wife says that she knows he is good to his employees. Whenever he talks in his sleep, for example, he says things like: ". . .and I will see you and raise you fifty dollars!"

THE JOKE OF SUPERIORITY

Here the joke is on someone else in a situation we feel "could never happen to me" or "I'm too smart for that." We believe ourselves insulated from the problem and, from the safety of our cozy room, we can watch without remorse while someone we don't know slips on the banana peel.

Example: Harry thinks he has class because he spent $100 on the best seats to see *Swan Lake.* Then he complained that he still couldn't hear a word they said.

THE JOKE OF INCONGRUITY AND EXAGGERATION

The joke in this case depends upon the impossible, or at least unlikely, combination of otherwise common ideas and events which seem to take on a life of their own as they "snowball" and grow. It could never have happened, but accepting the premise that it happened anyway, here's how it might have ended.

Example: Harry really led a tough life, and it shows. One Sunday he went to St. Michael's and the pastor was thundering at the congregation, "you must all pay the price of your sins!" Then he spotted Harry and added: "Those who have already paid the price of their sins may disregard this notice."

THE JOKE OF SURPRISE

The favorite example of this joke style is the Jack-in-the-Box or the compressed snakes in the peanut brittle can. The listener is led down what seems to be a familiar and safe path that ends instead in a totally unexpected way. The listener is surprised and amused by the unexpected twist.

Example: Harry has worked here a long time and one day I asked him what he had done with all the money he had earned. He thought for a moment and said, "I spent quite a bit on women, drink, gambling, entertainment . . . and the rest I spent foolishly."

THE JOKE OF THE PUNCTURED PRETENSION

The experts say that humor can be corrective when used as a vehicle to make a point that might otherwise be too dangerous to try for (. . . "many a word spoken in jest, etc . . . ."). This joke tries to deflate the inflated and is often the latest political joke which society may use in seeking revenge upon the Establishment.

Example: I had three topics given me to select from tonight. The first was "Harry: A Manager for the '80s" (pause, then rip paper).

The second was "Harry: A Warm and Sensitive Human Being" (pause, then rip paper).

And the third one, which I finally selected, "Harry: The Man and His Music."

THE JOKE OF RELIEF, OR
THE PASSING OF A STRAIN

Here we can laugh at some narrow escape or the final resolution of what could have been a fearful experience or nasty episode.

Example: I'm glad Harry is with us tonight . . . as we very nearly lost him today in a collision. It seems his boss stopped at the coffee machine without signaling and Harry rear-ended him.

The variations are as endless as snowflakes or grains of sand upon the beach. We think it helps a little to understand the tools of our trade but, as Mark Twain warned us, attempting to define humor is a bit like dissecting the flower to learn why it blooms; when you have it all pulled apart, you are not really sure what you have, and you have killed the poor thing in the process.

What is our definition of humor? It is whatever makes you laugh with enjoyment and without embarrassment or pressure.

What may be more relevent than a definition is an understanding of what goes into making up the Roast or, better yet, the successful Roast.

We are reminded of our good business friend, Ernie. He was one of the nicest people and the worst joke teller that either of us ever met in our entire business career.

Ernie couldn't tell a joke, but he told them anyway. First

he invariably set the stage for one of his unfunny offerings by alienating his audience with the warning that ".....This is only funny if you have a sense of humor." The joke hasn't been minted yet that could survive that introduction, and Ernie once again buried himself as he so richly deserved.

Very bad judgment, Ernie, but a good observation all the same. The very first ingredient of a successful Roast is people with . . .

A SENSE OF HUMOR

It all starts with the guest of honor. You must in each case have a guest who has humor and is both agreeable and able to handle the incoming rounds of verbal abuse with a certain amount of tolerance, good grace, and panache. It also helps if said guest can generate the sort of restrained fury which leads folks to deduce that when the moment is right, Harry will fire a few salvos of his own.

A WELL-KNOWN SUBJECT

Another guest of honor issue and an important one. One of the many reasons your audience will attend is their identification with the subject, Harry. In this case, familiarization breeds humor; without it not much is funny. This is why people do not laugh at "in" jokes. They say "I don't get it" which means they don't identify, can't understand, and don't find it funny. Your guest must be well-known enough to bring it off or you have chosen the wrong recognition vehicle. If they don't know that Harry, the lawyer, likes to come in at 10:00 A.M. and leave by 4:00 P.M. they won't find anything funny in your announcement that: " . . . the company just installed the new boiler under Harry's office; that way if it explodes before 10:00 A.M. or after 4:00 P.M. no one will get hurt."

TOPICAL, RELEVANT, FUNNY MATERIAL

You will find a lot more on this subject in the "Writers, Writers, and Writers" section, but let us emphasize again just how important good material is to the successful Roast. You cannot succeed without it. There was a memoir written during the 1960s by an American businessman who had done consulting work for the Japanese after World War II. He recalled how he had begun one talk before a group of Japanese business people with a fairly long, and very American, shaggy dog story. It took him a few minutes to get the whole thing out while his interpreter stood by patiently. When he had finished his story the interpreter bowed, turned to the audience, and said a very few words at the conclusion of which the audience went into gales of appreciative and unrestrained laughter. Later that day, the American asked his interpreter exactly what he had said. "I did not know how to tell your story," the Japanese answered, "so I said 'our guest has just told a funny story, please laugh.'"

Since you don't have this man's advantage or resources you must strive to be amusing.

While we are on the general subject, a word about off-color or "blue" material. Like the old vaudeville comic in baggy pants, who could always get a cheap laugh by dropping them, there is a time and a place for off-color humor. That place may be a stag party or a smoker but it is not a public or business Roast with mixed genders, generations, and personal guests in attendance. If you feel you must use it, remember at least that it is a rich spice and must be used sparingly lest the laughter you provoke be the nervous laughter of embarrassment rather than the rich laughter of enjoyment.

COMPETENT PRESENTERS

You need a small group of willing workers to help you find, write, and rewrite the Roast material. If they are the presenters, they must also agree to put in the time necessary for rehearsal. In an excellent article in *Toastmaster* magazine, writer/speaker Thomas Montalbo reminds us of Will Rogers' penetrating commentary on the subject: "The guys that tell you they can be funny at any minute, without any effort, are guys that ain't funny to anybody but themselves." Thank you, Will.

As for the rehearsal, it is a must. Your presenters must become familiar (and comfortable) with the material, get the timing right (allowing for laughs, for example, so they don't step on their own best material), and generally make sure that they fill their time slot with the best material available presented in the most professional manner of which they are capable. In a subsequent section we will discuss the use of audiotape, videotape, and even "mirrored" rehearsals.

REMEMBER YOU ARE STAGING AN ENTERTAINMENT

These points may seem self-evident but so many times Roast Masters seem to forget that:

1. No one came to watch another person be humiliated. Your audience came to enjoy themselves, share a little camaraderie and friendship in a congenial social gathering with perhaps the expectation of having a few chuckles at a friend's dented dignity and scratched ego, knowing that no real harm is intended or will be done.

2. The Roast is no place for personal causes. We all may have our own political and religious beliefs but the Roast is not the place or the vehicle through which to foist them off on the unsuspecting public. Some people will find it an irresistible temptation: a microphone and a captive audience. What a splendid opportunity to let everyone know what Tree Worship means to you, or how your faith as a Druid has carried you through

the dark times. Forget it, or as Archie Bunker said, "Stifle!" It is not the place or the time, no one cares to hear or wants to hear. Be in the spirit of the evening or be gone!

3. You must keep it moving. This is the job of the Master of Ceremonies and we'll talk about it in more detail later. For now, just remember to keep it in motion, eliminate dead air, cut short the bores, help out the faltering, and gag the hecklers.

4. This is a special occasion. Well, what is the occasion? Let's simulate one:

Our subject tonight is Harry Gordon. He might be in the process of promotion, transfer, or even retirement. We want to recognize Harry for his many years of service to the company and just for being a good friend. We have considered hosting a coffee hour, luncheon, cocktail party, dinner, informal presentation before his peers, and a Roast.

As we think our options through, we must consider one more hard and fast rule: whatever is happening to Harry Gordon, it must be positive and must be perceived by his peers as being positive. One does not do a Roast to commemorate demotions, relief from duty, or terminations (with extreme prejudice or otherwise). If you do not like Harry, wait for him in the parking lot and beat him up, but do not Roast him. It is certain to backfire and you will live to regret it.

Okay, whatever is happening to Harry is positive and everyone knows it. How about the rest of our ingredients?

Well, Harry is well-known for his own jokes and one-liners and has the ability to laugh at himself as well as at others. His sense of humor seems to be okay.

He is certainly well-known throughout the company—and not just because he has been here for twenty-seven years. After all, he could have been locked away in the back room somewhere, forecasting how many industrial angels will dance on next year's corporate pin, and none of us would even have known he was there. However, everybody knows our Harry Gordon.

We are doing well so far. We'll assume for the moment that we can handle the writing requirement and that we have the help we need. It is time to go see Harry.

We want to know if the idea of a Roast is agreeable to Harry and we will ask him so directly in a nonpressurized situation where he is free to answer as he will. We feel about surprise Roasts the way we used to feel about blind dates, people from the government who say they only want to help, and dentists who promise not to hurt. We will get out our Roast Profile Worksheet and go see Harry.

We will tell him directly what we are trying to accomplish and what we would like to do. We will ask him how he feels about a Roast and if he will freely agree to one. We will show him our Roast Profile Worksheet and explain it to him in detail with particular emphasis on the "Off Limits" section which he controls.

We may even agree to give him the closing slot—ten glorious minutes of rebuttal and revenge wherein Harry may torment the tormentors. We'll offer him the services of our best writers and promise him secrecy. We will get him involved in the planning, writing, and conducting of a rebuttal Roast all his own.

Have we got it all then? An agreeable well-known guest of honor with a sense of humor and a willingness to participate? A positive and suitable occasion? The people and other resources to write, rehearse, arrange, and produce it? The concept of an entertainment?

Does Harry agree to the idea?

Do we understand that people have come to have fun and to honor a friend? Good, then we won't spoil any part of it, nor will we allow others to do so. We'll remember that a Roast line should be to an insult what "wrassling" is to wrestling: a well-rehearsed and produced parody of lines and postures which create the illusion of conflict in a controlled setting, intended only to amuse and entertain.

Excellent! Now we can begin.

2

Planning and Preparation

When coauthor Ed McManus taught school for the Army, all novice instructors were routinely inducted into the philosophy of "The Five Ps":

PRIOR PLANNING PREVENTS POOR PERFORMANCE!

It was something like that, anyway. The point of the whole message was that nothing happens automatically correct and those who expect things to go "all right on the day" without prior planning, will go down to "the vile dust from which they sprung, unwept, unhonored, and unsung."

Let's examine the various planning steps and building blocks of the successful Roast.

THE ROAST COMMITTEE

Now that we have determined that all the necessary ingredients are present and that Harry Gordon is willing (even enthusiastic) about the Roast prospect, it is time to do what all good managers have done since the dawn of civilization: get a good, motivated team together, delegate, establish schedules, and follow up. Hence, the Roast Committee.

There is room for all sorts of different people on the Roast Committee. Naturally you will need writers, presenters, organizers and the like, but don't forget the publicity people, ticket sellers, decorations, transportation and the like. All of these ingredients play an essential part in the successful Roast. Let them all join and be recognized from the dais and on the program, as long as they have the one essential ingredient: a willingness to follow instructions and to meet schedules.

Remember that the Roast Committee is made up of the managers of each of the subcommittees which do most of the actual work. Let us review these subcommittees on an individual basis:

The Writers and Presenters Subcommittee

In many cases these are the same people, but, if they are not, they must work together very closely. They are responsible for establishing the Roast's length (usually an hour, sometimes 90 minutes; often less, never more), interviewing and recommending the presenters and working with them, and using the Roast Profile Worksheet to collect, write, and rewrite all the necessary material.

This group conducts the rehearsals, handles the timing, and at least recommends, if not selects, the Roast Master.

This subcommittee makes a major contribution and is one to stay in touch with on a regular and continuing basis to review accomplishments, solve problems, set schedules, and generally make sure the whole effort stays on time and on target.

The Function and Location Subcommittee

These people work with you to determine what sort of function will surround the Roast (luncheon, cocktails, dinner, etc.) and where it will be held. A dinner is always our first choice, but you must decide that based on the interest, time available, budget, etc. There is something basically positive about a group of friendly people sharing a meal and good fellowship that goes a long way toward insuring a successful evening.

This subcommittee will visit several potential Roast sites with their checklists, talk to the management, obtain quotations, analyze the competing offers, and make a recommendation to the Roast Committee on the type of function, where it should be held, the available dates, and the estimated cost per person.

Another caveat: Watch the dates! Make sure that they do not conflict with any other dates important to anyone involved in the Roast. We still tell the story of the meeting we were running at an exotic resort location, with several hundred people flying in from all over the world, when someone on our committee asked, "Why did you schedule the meeting on Passover when Jewish employees probably cannot attend?" It turned out that there was an error on the planning calendar we had used. It was wrong. We survived, learning one more important rule: Check the calendar for Easter and Passover, then call a local priest and rabbi to be sure.

Once the function has been decided on, and the location selected, keep this subcommittee in place. It can handle all necessary liaison with the location management, handle the setup and administration of the Roast, and handle whatever financial transactions there may be, through the final bill.

Tickets and Publicity

This unsung subcommittee gets the tickets printed and distributed to the various departments or other locations of sale and handles all such publicity as posters, mailers, local/in-house paper and radio announcements, bulletin board notices, and word-of-mouth. The publicity must begin immediately after the function, location, and date are set. It is this group's mission to insure that no one ever complains about their absence from the Roast by saying: "Oh, if I had only known. . . "

This group can probably do the program as well.

The Awards Subcommittee

This should be an easy one and may even be merged with some other subcommittee. If Harry is to get an award, and indeed he should, these people discuss the idea and come back with a list of suggested gifts like a pen set, clock, calculator, leather products, etc., for final committee decision.

Another aside: We have had people canvass family, friends, old newspaper and announcement files for pictures and clippings particularly important to Harry. Then we've had them made into a collage and framed with a caricature and notation of the Roast and its date. It makes a meaningful, unusual, and inexpensive gift.

Other places to look for gift awards include good jewelry stores, art and antique shops, and office supply firms. Check the Yellow Pages under "Awards," "Gifts," and "Trophies."

The secret of good committee work is good people, properly motivated, handling specific assignments with schedules to meet, and a feeling of freedom, authority, and contribution.

THE BUDGET

Yes, Virginia, Roasts do cost money and you should be prepared to pay for:

The Location

Another good reason for combining a Roast with a dinner is that in return for all those meals, and the bar, many restaurants will offer you the use of a private room at no charge and will probably let you use their sound system as well. These are two of the most expensive items on any Roast budget and although you must take care in the room selection (we will come to that later), for now it is enough to talk about getting such a room at no cost.

Just remember that it must be a private room, where all of your participants are free from the prying ears and eyes of strangers who will not understand much of what's going on anyway but whose very presence may intimidate your speakers who are willing enough to perform before friends, but not the general public. Get yourself a private room.

The Meal

An easy and customary Roast format is to begin the evening with an informal reception and cocktail hour with a cash bar (each person pays for himself). At a predetermined hour, notice is given and the entire group moves to the dinner tables for the evening meal.

Usually, the restaurant will have suggested narrowing the menu to two or three choices to simplify handling and keep the function on schedule. The reduced menu may include a meat, fish, and vegetarian dish but whatever you select, go with the reduced menu in the interests of time and simplicity.

The meal is most often paid for in advance through the attendee's purchase of the Roast ticket. The ticket price, then, would be the price of the dinner, plus tax and tip, along with a bit extra to cover a reasonable gift and whatever other expenses you may have incurred along the way (equipment rental, special transportation requirements, publicity costs, printing, etc.). Just remember to keep the ticket priced as reasonably as possible to insure that people who want to attend can afford to do so. The only exception to this rule would be the fund-raising Roast where the ticket price is further enlarged to allow for a contribution of "n" dollars (where "n" equals what the traffic will bear) to the campaign or subject cause.

The Sound System

This deserves a paragraph all to itself.

The reason professional musicians and other entertainers go to the time and expense of carrying their own sound system and technicians along with them will become clear to you the first time you hear the quality of some of the sound systems certain restaurant people will set up for you. Sometimes they are forty or more years old, dating back to the construction of the restaurant itself, and the quality of reproduction is similar to an old 78 rpm record you might pick up at a yard sale. Check out the sound system! Make sure the subcommittee in charge goes there and listens to it. Is there a nice, crisp, sound? Do you have your own volume control? Where else does it play within the property? Tell the management you want the sound confined to your private room. Also, ask if any other system or room plays over the same speakers. Nothing is more disruptive to any speaking function than broadcast music and chatter from some other room, or a hostess paging dinner reservations or calling John Doe to the phone while one of your speakers is trying to carry off his Roast.

If there is the slightest problem or concern with the restaurant system, forget about it and rent your own at a local TV/music shop. All you need is an amplifier, a couple of good speakers, and a microphone. Ask the committee if any of them has a personal sound system you could use. If someone has one, borrow it, and bring along a tape deck to use for background music during the reception, perhaps during dinner, and maybe even for dancing afterwards.

Another special note: If you decide to provide your own system, be sure to tell the restaurant, so they can turn off whatever normally plays in your room. Tell them to be sure their system is off, have someone check early on the night of the Roast to be sure it is, and consider carrying a small pair of side cutters and electrical tape so that, if necessary, you can perform an on-the-spot sound system lobotomy and wire it together again after.

The Gift

We have already discussed this and we suggest you do it. Remember, it is not the expense but the thoughtfulness and recognition that will count and be remembered. Many successful sales organizations have gotten miles and miles of use from a simple walnut plaque with a handsome plate on which is inscribed Harry's name and accomplishment, the date, and some pertinent quotation or sentiment to sum it all up. Do it well and Harry will keep it on his wall forever.

So, what should the budget be? It should be the sum

of the meal, tax, gratuity, gift, other administrative costs and, if appropriate, a donation to the cause.

Another aside: if you are running a fund-raising Roast, particularly for some local effort, don't hesitate to ask the restaurant for some little consideration to "help keep expenses down." Naturally you will acknowledge this from the podium and in the program.

3

The Roast Profile
Worksheet

It is interesting that all our successes seem to blend into one indistinguishable happy memory while each of our failures stands out in vivid nightmarish detail. I remember one Roast that was a particular disaster.

The subject was a local political figure and the Roast Masters felt that he was popular enough, and well-known enough, for people to write and present good, topical, relevant, funny material. The Roast Masters were wrong. Except for a few deft touches concerning some legislation he had sponsored, no one on the dais really knew the man. What was he like? Did he hunt or write poetry? Yale or hard knocks? Football or ballet? The Roast Masters didn't take the necessary time to think through in a logical order what they were trying to accomplish, or they would have realized that you can't take liberties with a background that you don't know; you can't parody an unspecified interest; you can't Roast a total stranger. The jokes they used were thin, general, irrelevant, flat, and (worst of all) not funny.

Enter the Roast Profile Worksheet (Exhibit 1). We will discuss what it is, why it is important, make sure you understand it, and then go through one for Harry along with a few examples.

The purpose of the Roast Profile Worksheet is to establish one central reference document on which we can collect and store for retrieval all the information we will need to collect, write, rewrite the material necessary for our successful Roast. Please take a look at the form now; it is on page 44.

Your first reaction may be something like "I cannot possibly collect all of that information." That's okay; just get as much of it as you can. What is important is that you start with the idea of proceeding in an orderly and organized fashion to collect in this one place all the facts you will need to draw from, and the personal data that will lead you to the Roast lines you want and need.

Your second reaction may be: "Where do I start?" The answer to that is easy; you start with Harry, the subject himself. Just remember that Harry has already agreed to the idea of a Roast and he will now be more than willing to cooperate with us for some very good reasons:

1. He will want to be sure you have your facts straight. If you are going to kid him about winning the Nobel Prize, he will want you to mention that it was in 1981, and in the field of Chemistry, and he was, of course, the sole winner.

2. He will want to have at least some input into the story you are assembling. Harry is human, and if you listen closely, he will lead you *to* certain areas and *away* from others. Let him offer, if he will, "the silk rope with which he will be strung up."

3. Since it is his evening, Harry will want to be a good sport and to be seen as one. Harry never does anything halfway and if he is going to be Roasted, he will want to have the biggest and best Roast of the year.

In addition to Harry, you may want to contact his wife, older children, friends, business associates, and whoever else you can think of who comes into contact with Harry on some sort of regular basis. Go for the blend of several different views from different people who know Harry from a variety of personal and business vantage points. Once the Roast is announced, you may find many of these people looking for you, anxious to get involved. Encourage them. The more contacts, the more data, the more relevant lines, the funnier and more successful Roast.

Let us take a detailed look at the sample Roast Profile Worksheet for our good friend, Harry Gordon, and we shall see just where it leads us. (*Note:* The Roast lines at the back of the book are tied to the Roast Profile Worksheet paragraph numbers for fast reference.)

Paragraphs 1, 2, and 3 are simply name, address, and telephone information blanks. There is usually not much material from here, but in this case, noting Harry's "Harmony Road" address and his musical interests, we might suggest that Harry's address, like rich food, hardly ever agrees with him. Better material follows.

Paragraph 4 asks about Harry's age. If you cannot get it exactly, estimate it as closely as possible. Since Harry is over fifty, we might suggest that ". . . he is a mature business thinker; all his best ideas are over thirty years old." That line would not work if Harry was in his late twenties. However, if Harry was an Engineering Vice President in his late twenties, that would lead to youth jokes like "It is impossible to see Harry between one and three any afternoon; his secretary makes him nap"; or "How would you feel about taking technical leadership from a guy whose breath reeked of Twinkies?"

Age is a very important source of joke material if you consider some historical event that took place in the subject's lifetime and give him some part in it. How about "Harry remembers two things about Will Rogers. He remembers Will saying 'I never met a man I didn't like,' and he remembers Will punching him out. (Pause). It wasn't a fair fight, though. Harry said Dale Carnegie was holding his arms."

Paragraph 5 inquires about Harry's wife's name as well as the names and ages of his children. This sort of detail can lead us to bachelor/family humor, children, and domestic joke material. We see that there is a Harry Jr., aged twenty-four. How about "His namesake, Harry Jr., is the spitting image of his old man. Oh well, as long as the boy is healthy."

Also, "Harry's wife, Doris, showed me the diamond ring Harry bought her. I told her how beautiful it is and she said 'Yes, but it comes with the Gordon Curse.' I said 'Gordon

Curse? What's the Gordon Curse?' She said, 'Harry.' "

Paragraph 6, education, schools, and degrees, is one of the richer sources of joke information. Just about everybody is vulnerable here. Harry has an Engineering degree from Texas A&M which you might suggest is "the equal of any secondary school in the country"; how about "Aggie only gives Engineering degrees to the guys who can't make the team."

Harry also has an MBA from Harvard. That might suggest "Not everyone from Boston goes to Harvard; if you know the right people you can get out of it." You could try for a blend with "His family hoped Harry would get the best of both worlds: a Harvard education and Aggie common sense. Unfortunately for us all, Harry got an Aggie education and Harvard common sense."

Paragraph 7 deals with his jobs, past and present. Harry is an Engineering Vice President, which suggests "He's so technical that sometimes he can't speak"; or he might be "one of the few guys in the company today who can do the nine-times-table from memory." Just maybe "Harry won't give up the old slide rule though; he uses it to push the buttons on his computer console."

In Harry's previous life as a consultant did he really "advise Fortune 500 firms on how to defy the Industrial Revolution"? Maybe Harry "wanted to be a consultant for our firm too but it didn't work out; we saw him every day."

Have they heard about "the old lady who had her tomcat fixed to stop it from going out every night? Well, it still went out every night thereafter, but just as a consultant."

You might remind your audience that "Consultants take on intricate research projects that most average folks cannot understand—like worrying about whether Darwin's birthday should be a religious holiday for apes."

Paragraph 8 deals with personal characteristics; "how to win friends and influence people." "Harry's ego was so high that for years he believed that when he died, the Trinity would become a Quartet."

Let us hope that "Harry does not believe he's Superman just because he was once picked up for undressing in a phone booth."

Perhaps we can prove what sort of a dresser he is "by looking at the labels on his suits: Hart, Schaffner, and Rescue Mission #7."

Maybe you will tell them about Harry "joining Exercise Anonymous. You call them whenever you're tempted to exercise and they send someone over to drink with you until the urge passes."

Paragraph 9, service background, can be a lot of fun when you couple it with Harry's age and his time of service. You often find that the executive of today was the private of yesteryear. Harry was a truck driver. Was that a result of "the Army's recognizing his full management potential" or was it simply "the last job he ever had that he could handle"?

The World War II vet is begging for lines like "he was once nearly court-martialed for excessive buffalo hairs on his saddle" or "failure to turn out for formation in correct and fully polished armor." We often like to look at our notes and report to the audience that "Harry was a veteran of World War II but, unfortunately, the notes don't specify which side he was on."

Paragraph 10 asks about home, and Harry is from Dallas, Texas. Maybe that explains why he "has all the warmth and charm of a Southern Sheriff."

Someone should ask Harry if it's true that "you can tell a Texan's age by counting the sweat rings in his hat."

How about admitting to the audience that we always know "when Harry has gone home to Texas for a while; for the first few weeks after he comes back he is virtually unintelligible."

Paragraph 11, weekends and vacations, probably should be read together with Paragraph 12, personal interests, for maximum effect. Harry likes to read; good. Couple that with his dislike of exercise, and we learn that "It's good that Harry likes to read so much; moving his lips is about the only exercise he ever gets."

Harry likes to play the violin because "he wins every time."

He might even be considering a change to the piano "because his drinks keep slipping off the violin."

If Harry is a bachelor, maybe his interest in archaeology explains "some of the dates he's dug up."

And don't forget about his "spending $100 on tickets to the ballet and then complaining because he still couldn't hear a word they said."

How about interests like photography ("We're always reminding him: 'Harry, glass side towards the subject' ") or golf ("I told him about this guy on a golf course who went berserk and beat his partner to death with his golf club; Harry said 'How many strokes?' ")? How Harry spends his time and what he likes to do gives both a good view of the real Harry and also opens a valuable vein of good source material.

Paragraph 13 deals with more serious stuff—philosophy. Maybe "the main difference between Harry and Socrates is that after you hear Harry's philosophy, you want to drink from the poison cup."

Or, "many a wise word has been spoken in jest, Harry, but for sheer volume they can't compete with the number of stupid words you have said in earnest."

Perhaps we could sum it all up by telling our audience that "the good news is that Harry's finest piece of philosophy is 'Do it now, do it right, and be done with it.' The bad news is that that really is Harry's finest piece of philosophy."

Paragraph 14 deals with achievements and awards. How about "that Army Unit Citation was presented by President Roosevelt himself—and Teddy didn't give an award to just anybody."

Perhaps "we once asked Harry if he had considered signing a contract with the Book of the Month Club and he said, 'No, I could never write a book a month.' "

Maybe Harry "likes to write about old-fashioned values like Integrity and Honor; in fact, whenever the local library gets a book on either of those subjects, Harry steals it."

Paragraph 15 is for special comments and remarks that

need to be made but just do not fit anywhere else. "There was the time a local religious leader sat in on one of Harry's staff meetings, and when it was over he told Harry his meetings were 'like the Peace of God and the Love of God both.' Harry was so pleased, he asked the man why. 'Because,' the religious leader said, 'the Peace of God surpasses all understanding, and the Love of God endures forever.'"

"What's this threat about Harry avenging himself tonight? Is that like being challenged to a battle of wits with an unarmed man?" or "We could make it into a movie if Hollywood hadn't already used *The Mouse That Roared.*"

How about those staff meetings that end up at the Pub? Is it true that "Harry's department stopped off to donate blood on the way home one day, and the Red Cross used it to sterilize their instruments."

How about the Friday afternoon we had "the big thunderstorm and six of Harry's guys tried to lash him to the bar?"

And of course there are always the good old general lines like "Harry may be outspoken, but I don't know by whom"; or "Harry never touched a thing that didn't belong to him in the twenty-three years he has been here; he's always been watched too closely."

Finally, tell them that "Harry's not a 'yes' man; when the boss says 'no,' Harry will say 'no' too."

Paragraph 16 is what Harry considers "Off Limits." If our purpose is to recognize, amuse, and entertain, we want to give Harry a chance to state for the record just what is beyond the pale. In Harry's case, it's wife or girlfriend jokes and blue material. No harm done; let's observe his wishes. The Roast Profile Worksheet has given us enough source material for several Roasts without crossing that boundary line of taste and embarrassment that might have Harry and your audience squirming in their seats and praying for the hands of the clock to move just a bit faster.

Now let us look back over the material we have collected from the Roast Profile Worksheet and see how it led us to the joke categories in the back of the book. All we really need to ice the cake is a good introduction and a strong close, both of which are detailed in this book.

With a little thought, insight, work, and skill, along with the Roast Profile Worksheet to focus your attention, you are well on your way to researching and writing a very successful Roast for good old Harry Gordon.

EXHIBIT 1
ROAST PROFILE WORKSHEET

1. Subject's Name: _____
2. Address: _____
3. Phone: Home: _____ Office: _____
4. Age: _____ 5. Family (Names and Ages): _____
_____

6. Education (Schools and Degrees): _____
_____
_____

7. Position (Title, Employer, Duration): Current: _____
_____
    Previous: _____
8. Personal Characteristics: _____
_____

9. Service Background (Branch, Rank, Dates, Accomplishments): _____
_____

10. Where Does Subject Consider "Home": _____
_____

11. What Does Subject Do on Weekends? Vacations? _____
_____
_____

12. Personal Interests (Double XX If Avid): _____
__Golf   __Hunting   __Theatre
__Tennis   __Camping   __Movies
__Squash   __Photography   __Collector (of _____)
__Running   __Reading   __Musician (Instr: _____)
__Fishing   __Painting   __Other _____
13. Subject's Personal/Business Philosophy (Typical Quote): _
_____
_____

14. Subject's Proudest Achievement (This Year?) (Ever?): ___
_____

15. Special Comments: _____
_____
_____

16. OFF LIMITS: _____
_____

4

Casting and Timing

It has been said that some people cannot tell a joke. This may not be 100 percent true but, as many contractors from the military-industrial complex will tell you: "It's close enough for government work."

The reality of the situation is that joke-telling, like singing, is an acquired skill. Almost everybody likes to sing at one time or another, and most of us can carry a tune to the point where it can be recognized by a friend trying desperately hard to recognize it. With a few lessons and a little effort, in fact, most people can develop their vocal skills until they are qualified to sing in church or temple choirs, choral groups, and similar non-solo endeavors. In fact, as we listen to the Top Forty shatter its way from eardrum to eardrum, we might even make a case for claiming that certain professionals really can't sing at all.

Like singing, learning to tell a joke properly is an acquired skill, and those who are willing to work at it a little can learn to carry off a story well enough to satisfy the intent of any social or business Roast. In fact, sometimes the funniest and most popular Roast participants are those unlikely folk, known more for their grave and stern countenance, than for any comedic skills. These are the folks who can knock an audience dead simply because so little is expected of them. Remember that two of humor's more important ingredients are surprise and incongruity, and what could be more incongruous or surprising than some grim and humorless Cotton Mather type facing an audience with his bleak visage broadcasting the evil of fun, and he begins with:

"Harry's philosophy speaks to the Ages—the Ages between eight and fourteen."

So you must bring to the casting effort an open mind and a willingness to be surprised. You'll get most of your leads by contacting the people closest to your subject and soliciting both suggestions and volunteers. Then, after a few informal interviews, you can make your selection based on their agreements to (1) submit a written outline of what they intend to say or do by some mutually agreeable date, (2) observe the guidelines as established by the Roast Profile Worksheet, (3) rehearse on their own and conduct at least one dress rehearsal with you, (4) appear on the day, at the time, in proper order, and (5) submit to the leadership and direction of the Roast Master or Master of Ceremonies. Let's go through these important points in more detail, one at a time.

THE SUBMISSION OF A WRITTEN OUTLINE

This requirement affords you the opportunity to both help and control. It helps you judge the participants' abilities to operate on their own, lets you see if they can actually construct such an outline, what it looks like of course, and helps you decide just how much help they are going to need. It assures you that something will get done on paper by a certain date, and thus allow you some reaction (or panic) time if you should need it. You must remember Will Rogers' warning about the people who don't feel they need any special preparation. That's just someone's ego talking and without your involvement and leadership, they will fail.

OBSERVE THE GUIDELINES OF
THE ROAST PROFILE WORKSHEET

In addition to being a gold mine of source material for comments and funny lines, the Roast Profile Worksheet will also advise what is out of bounds and or taboo. Your would-be Roaster must agree to such boundaries despite his feeling that a line on some much forbidden subject would be great fun anyway. It might be great fun for him, but not for your guest or for your audience.

We like to tell Roaster candidates about the foreman who was watching two production line workers come very close to having a fight. Every so often, one would jiggle a little piece of string in front of the other, who would react with great curses and threats of violence. Sensing the imminent explosion, the foreman collared the first worker and demanded an explanation. "Oh," said the worker, "just a little fun with no harm intended. His brother was hanged yesterday and I was just kidding him about it." Stick with your guidelines!

REHEARSAL ON THEIR OWN AND AT LEAST ONCE WITH YOU

Again, this is a control measure and enables you to learn what they are doing and how well it is coming along. Insist on these rehearsals. People who tell you not to worry, "I'll bring it off on the night" do not bring it off on the night. They die—and the Roast dies with them. They must rehearse and, if they're nervous, tell them to do it for a while with just a mirror for company. Get a cassette recorder and offer to tape their presentation and play it back to them in private. If you are in a large corporation or institution, you might even make arrangements with your audio-visual department to put their rehearsal on videotape.

Have you ever seen yourself on videotape? What an eye-opener that is. Each and every empty move, flat line and meaningless gesture is caught by the cruel eye of the camera as you sit there and squirm, watching yourself in action, and praying for it all to end, mercifully soon.

I recommend that you offer to tape each Roaster once at the very start of his rehearsals and again towards the end.

Let him see the improvement which has come from effort, content, delivery, and timing.

Another stage whisper: all of this rehearsal business gives you a splendid chance to weed out unfunny or objectionable material under the guise of "that one fell flat, it's not you, we should cut it." Always keep a few good lines about so you can help with the substitution or just flesh out the presentation.

One final thought on rehearsals: I once worked on a Roast where one of the participants was a very important man (and he'd tell you so himself if you didn't notice). We had tried several times to get him to rehearsals, but each and every time we were rebuffed by schedule conflicts, travel arrangements, and the like. We finally let him off the hook; we told him he need not attend any rehearsals. This made him very happy until the night of the Roast. He was long and unfunny, stumbled over his own lines, stepped on the few good stories he had, and generally made a fool of himself. Later in the evening he told us: "This was your fault. If you had done your job properly and made me rehearse for this Roast, I know I would have done a much better job."

Moral: No one likes to look bad in front of peers and associates. To guard against that, you must alert all of the participants to the danger and insist that they rehearse.

APPEARING ON THE DAY, AT THE TIME, IN PROPER ORDER

This may all seem self explanatory, but you must warn people, especially busy people, not to volunteer unless they are prepared to make the commitment. Most people will understand and appreciate your message. If they are traveling, for example, ask them to return the evening before for the final rehearsal, and to avoid the plane that always seems to run an hour late, or the road that leads through a congested tunnel.

"In proper order" means simply that their head cavities

must be filled with functioning gray matter and not with alcohol-drenched marshmallows. A mumbling, falling down drunk may be funny for a very few moments, but he can't bring the lines off and, as soon as he realizes that people are laughing *at* him and not *with* him, he may even grow hostile. Once someone starts rocking the Roast boat, you may never stabilize it again. I ask people to consider the Roast in the same serious context as a business presentation or serious club speech and to conduct themselves accordingly.

Another subtle way to gain control in these matters is to arrange to have the Roast room available to you for a few hours before the Roast itself begins. Invite people in for a final rehearsal and to "get the feel of the room." Tell them this will be their last chance to try out the sound system and become familiar with the setting. Tell them that everything from the sound system to the lights will be live and "on," and that you will be there to help insure that they present themselves and their material in the best possible fashion.

Again, people want to look good and want to do a good job. They will most often submit to leadership extended to them under such a reasonable offer of help.

SUBMITTING TO THE LEADERSHIP OF THE MASTER OF CEREMONIES OR ROAST MASTER

Every participant must understand that the MC, or RM, is the captain of the team. His signals must be followed in all cases. This person will introduce the speakers, egg them on as necessary, calm them down as appropriate, shorten their presentation where required, and generally get them on and off for their own benefit and for the benefit and success of the Roast itself. All participants must agree to accept the RM's judgment and guidance concerning the conduct of the evening in general, and the Roast in particular.

Casting, then, simply means finding the right people and working with them to insure they succeed.

As for Timing, there are two aspects of Timing to consider now which can affect the Roast and its ability to achieve the goals you have set out for it.

The first aspect to consider is the timing of the Roast itself. How long should it be? How long should the individual presentations be? If you ask two different people to do ten minutes and just leave them to their own devices, the first person will do five minutes and the second will do thirty minutes. If you are not careful, you could have the same problem with your introductions and transitions, and what you intended to be a one-hour romp will have turned into a three-hour forced march.

How to control the timing? Is the whole really equal to the sum of its parts? The answer is no. The synergy of the inscrutable clock dictates that the whole is anywhere up to twice the sum of its parts—and increasing.

Let's start with the building block of the Roast: the individual presenter. At the outset, you tell each presenter that you want him to do between eight and ten minutes. That doesn't sound like much and he may tell you so. Then, you inform him that each minute should hold between two and four jokes, depending on their length. This means that each ten-minute segment requires twenty to forty excellent lines. Tell him that you will be very satisfied if he will deliver just the ten-minute block.

With your ten-minute speaker module and a two-minute Roast Master module, you have filled twelve minutes. Now add a 25-percent fit factor and you have accounted for about fifteen Roast minutes per presenter. How long should a Roast be? We think forty-five minutes to an hour is about right, with ninety minutes being an absolute outside limit. This means that technically you could do a forty-five minute Roast with three people, or a one-hour Roast with four people. Of course, it never works out that way.

What you will find on the night is that people, even rehearsed people, get nervous. Nervous people talk fast, and without intervention will move through their material much faster than either of you expected. The Roast Master might try to slow them down. A better solution is to have extra speakers prepared and ready to go. We recommend having one extra for every three speakers scheduled. You can always work them in somewhere, and it is a great comfort to see the dais filled with qualified speakers, scrubbed and tubbed and ready to go.

The second aspect of timing to consider is the timing involved in the telling of a story or the delivering of a line, as mentioned earlier. This knowledge, gained from instruction, practice, intuition, and rehearsal, tells the speaker when to speed up to get through certain less desirable material, and when to slow down to savor the impact of the good bits. It is the key to a successful presentation. When to pause for the laugh; when to deliver the topper; all this comes from your interaction with the presenter, from rehearsals taped and otherwise, and through the talents and stewardship of the Roast Master.

Finally, work closely with the Roast Master. Share and discuss your concerns and observations. Make sure he too has a script, has rehearsed, and understands his mission as Roast Master and team captain.

The bottom line then is to build your timing from the individual presenter through the Roast Master's introductions and transitions, to the end of the Roast where old Harry himself turns presenter and delivers the final module.

Casting and Timing are merely the proper use of the Roast resources.

5

The Roast: Writers, Writers, Writers

FINDING THE FUNNY STORY

Many would-be Roast Masters wither and turn cold at this critical point: finding the funny story. They may say that they don't have the time, don't know where to look, are not good at that sort of thing, or all three and a few more not mentioned. Don't worry. This sort of initial reaction is very natural, very common, and with the right sort of attitude and direction, very curable. We will find the necessary good material and, having decided that, should probably start by reviewing the available resources.

From the Roast Profile Worksheet, we already know the general subject areas and slants we want for Harry. We know his background, where he's vulnerable for a deft touch, and where to leave him alone. All well and good. Let's get into the resources.

Networking

Let everybody know that a Roast is coming up and that Harry will be the Guest of Honor. Tell them that you would welcome suitable material, and that if their material is used, they'll get a program mention under "Writers, Writers, Writers." Ask them to type or print their stories on three-by-five-inch file cards, one to a card, along with their names, and then drop off the finished products at your office for review. Encourage them to be original, to take a fresh view, and, if necessary, offer them a few hints on direction from the Roast Profile Worksheet.

Radio and Television

These are marvelous sources of new, funny, and topical material. That radio disc jockey you hear on the way to work probably subscribes to one of the best professional joke services in the country. Small local stations and off-hours broadcasters are probably the best source because fewer people are likely to have heard them, but don't walk away from any good line you hear. Even if you can't use it as is, you might be able to salvage it by rewriting it.

Example: One story suggested for Harry mentioned that early in his career, he had been one of the Three Stooges. It had been on a popular radio show, many people had heard it, it wasn't particularly funny or relevant, but it had a funny premise. We rewrote it along these lines: "When Harry joined the firm, he came highly recommended by his former employers. Larry, Moe, and Curly each wrote him a super reference."

On television, of course, professionals like Johnny Carson have some of the best, and highest paid, comedy writers in the business. These writers have to crank out enough material each viewing week to brighten up four or five broadcasting hours. A week's output like that would have lasted the entire career of a comic working in vaudeville years ago. It is generally high-grade, mass-produced humor, and its only major disadvantage to you is that a lot of other people who follow your viewing schedule will have heard it before. Rewrite it as necessary and take the chance. In the first place, most people can't remember a joke longer than a few hours after they have heard it anyway (how many times have you heard a friend chortle over some lines he heard the previous night and, although he remembers the lines being screamingly funny, he cannot remember a single one?), and in the second place, a joke refreshed or rewritten, and made relevant to Harry, becomes, for all practical purposes, an entirely new joke.

Now this does not mean you can sit up and copy Johnny

Carson word for word. It would probably not be legal; it would certainly not be fair; you most likely could not find a presenter to carry the whole thing off; it would definitely not be relevant to Harry and, worst of all, your audience would not think it was funny.

Always remember the old maxim about "borrowed" material: when you take from just one source, it's plagiarism; when you take from many sources, it's research.

Old Joke Books and Records

You will find these at flea markets, yard and garage sales, church bazaars, and (our favorite source) old book stores. They contain a treasure trove of funny information. Since people price what they sell by what it means to them, we have paid as little as a dime for some of the best material in our library.

You tried some of that you say, but the jokes were just too old and dated to be used at Harry's Roast? Wrong! One of the first things you must understand about humor is that there is no such thing as an old joke. The treatment and background may be dated but the humorous ingredient is ageless; it just needs a little refreshing. Here are two anecdotes for your consideration:

Around 1739, a little book of jokes started making the rounds of London coffee houses and such other places where the "smart set" of the time may have gathered. The book was called *Joe Miller's Jests; Or, The Wit's Vade-Mecum.* It was a slim little book containing 247 of the more popular stories in circulation. The stories (jokes, basically) were already old when they were published.

What helped to make the book so popular was that the book itself was a joke—an "in" joke among the clever folk, whom everyone wanted to emulate. The joke was this: Joe Miller didn't write the book. In fact, he was about the most humorless fellow you can imagine and probably could not even read or write.

Joe Miller (whose real first name was Joseph, Josias,

or Jonah) was a popular actor of the time who was renowned for his inability to be funny, or even interesting, without a script in his hand. Joe was an introverted, moody sort of chap who went to all the smart places but hung off in a corner by himself, always looking as if his best friend had just died.

The clever folk began attributing funny stories to Joe, and those who knew him found it amusing to even suggest that Joe knew, let alone could tell, a funny story. The idea caught on and Joe's manufactured reputation inspired a "put on" of the first order.

Naturally, when a man named John Mottley decided to collect the current funny stories into a book, he thought it would be great fun to attribute the whole thing to poor, gloomy, old Joe Miller. He did just that, and history was taken in on yet another bit of harmless nonsense.

The book was copied and republished so many times that it took on a life of its own and any overtold or stale joke came to be known as a "Joe Miller."

Recently, while making our rounds of the book sales, we bought for one dollar an interesting little book entitled: *Elegant Anecdotes – Original & Selected* by Perseval Adams, M. A.. The book was published in Glasgow by Napier and Khull in 1799. Perhaps the book is old enough to prove the point.

Another of our patented asides: Before we go too deeply into our example, note that the title of the book . . . *Original & Selected* suggests that our Mr. Adams drew at least some of his elegant anecdotes from an even earlier source. Since our attorneys advise that it has been years since Mr. Adams sued anyone, we suggest that he may have borrowed an old anecdote or two from the Joe Miller book published 60 years before.

Anyway, the following little story is reproduced here exactly as written. Remember to read an "f" as though it were an "s."

A perfon who was, fome years ago, accufed of robbing the Irifh treafury, went to the above Counfellor, to fee him to plead in his defence. "Well, my dear," fays the Counfellor, "and what have you done?" "Done," fays the other, "I have done nothing; but I am accufed of robbing the treafury." "By my own foul," (replys the Counfellor), "you were in the right on't, to go where the money was."

There it is, your basic 200-year old joke! Probably not usable? Wrong again! You have surely heard several versions of this same premise in a variety of different and more modern ways if you stop to think about it.

How about switching (or rewriting, or refreshing) it along these lines: "Harry finally explained to his kids why Robin Hood only stole from the rich—they were the only ones with anything worth stealing."

The same basic joke, with just a flip.

Remember the late 1960s when the bank robber Willie Sutton was in the news? When they asked Willie why he devoted his adult life to robbing banks, he allegedly replied: "Because that's where they keep the money." No need to thank Mr. Adams. He probably got it from a source which got it from a source who had read it on a papyrus scroll reporting the interrogation of an Egyptian grave robber nabbed by the troops of Amenhotep III which read ". . . and when the desert vermin was questioned by the Chamberlain as to why he would despoil Pharaoh's tomb, he responded, 'For that is where the gold is found.' " We wonder where *he* got it.

And how does Mr. Adams' anecdote help out with Harry's Roast? Well, remember the day you asked Harry why he had spent his entire thirty-five year career working in the Finance Department? Harry said, "Because that is where they keep the money."

Yard sales, bazaars, and the like can be important sources of good material but the old book stores deserve a few paragraphs all to themselves.

You'll find these stores in the yellow pages, the classified section of your local newspaper, or maybe you even pass one on the way to and from work and have always meant to stop in but somehow never found the time. Now is the time. Allow yourself a minimum of thirty minutes for your first trip to talk with the owners, savor the atmosphere, and just browse.

Start with a chat and tell the operators that you are looking for old joke books, one-liners, toasts, speakers' anthologies, etc., and let them take it from there.

You may be interested to learn that after-dinner speeches, the precursor of the more modern Roast, were a popular form of evening entertainment among the upper middle classes during the last century both in America and Europe. Politicians, writers, humorists, and even motivational speakers were as active on this circuit as they are today, playing then, perhaps, to even larger crowds who did not have the luxury of alternate forms of entertainment to choose from.

Mark Twain was very big on this circuit. He was once preceded on the program by a pompous local attorney who chided Twain for speaking with his hands in his pockets, and expressed the hope that Mr. Twain would rise above this nasty habit tonight. Twain, when it was his turn, responded by noting the attorney's profession and suggested that at least he, Twain, only put his hands into his *own* pockets. William Jennings Bryan was paid up to $700 an evening for speeches like his "Cross of Gold" classic and that sum, in today's money, is right up there with what we pay our most popular entertainers.

You may find several good books from this period for anything from one to five dollars and not too much more. Buy them and treat yourself to an evening's entertainment, sharing jabs and one-liners with the better minds of another age, while you collect some classics with which to bury Harry.

And while you are there, be sure to check the paperback section for some good buys on jokes from the Fifties and Sixties, and check the magazine section for old joke magazines and the like. Then go through the old record section where you may find reissues of W. C. Fields, Fred Allen, and some contemporary comedy figures such as Bob Newhart, George Carlin, or Carl Reiner and Mel Brooks doing one of their "2000-Year Old Man" classics.

Finally, before you leave, give your name and address to the manager and ask to be notified about any new arrivals of material in your fields of interest.

Buy, read, listen—get ideas!

The Library

Most of us are card carrying members of all the libraries that surround our home towns and which we can convientiently visit on some sort of regular basis, like once each month. For a cost-effective way of finding good material at zero expense, your local library has no equal.

You should consider that multi-card idea. It generally costs nothing, and each card gives you access to a whole new selection committee with different views and, oh yes, a whole new municipal budget with which to buy books. Get yourself to a library.

To do it right and save yourself a lot of research time, you should understand how to use the library. The best way to do that is to ask someone at the desk for a good and straightforward book on the subject of using the library for reference purposes. The second best way to accomplish your goal is to have a chat with the librarian or research clerk along the very same lines as the one you had with the manager of the old book store. The third best way is to read this chapter and understand at least a little bit about the Dewey Decimal System.

Briefly, nearly every library is broken into classification sections in accordance with the Dewey Decimal System, developed by Melvil Dewey many years ago. His system, still in use today, separates all published material into ten main or subject classes, which are marked prominently on the bookshelves themselves. In general, we want the numbers between 800 and 899—the Literature and Rhetoric Section.

Although this first cut narrows the field down a bit, it is still a very broad area, and if you are pressed for time, you may not have the luxury of just browsing and picking up whatever suits your fancy. Therefore, the good Mr. Dewey and his obliging system further breaks the field down into subsections such as 817 (Satire and Humor) and 827 (English Satire and Humor).

There are, however, other numbers that could be relevant, and to keep things simple, we strolled around a couple of nearby libraries and found these sorts of books under the numbers shown:

Dewey Decimal Number	What We Found
400 Languages	Look closely at subsections 422 and 437 for word books, puns, comic dictionaries, etc.
700 The Arts	Under 741.59, we found cartoon collections by artists (like Charles Addams), and magazines (like *Esquire* and *The New Yorker*).
800 Literature and Rhetoric	808.5 has toasts, speakers' reference books, public speaking guides, etc.
	808.8 has quotations, great and sometimes funny thoughts, and bits of wisdom.
	808.87 has jokes, anecdotes, and one-liners.
	817 has novels and essays by Thurber, Allen (Fred and Woody), et al.
	827 English satire, stories, anecdotes, etc.

Depending on whether or not your audience shares a common ethnic heritage, you might also want to check the following stacks as well:

837   German Satire and Humor

847   French Satire and Humor

857   Italian Satire and Humor

867   Spanish Satire and Humor

877   Latin Satire and Humor

887   Classical Greek Satire and Humor

Somewhere between Latin and Classical Greek you might even find, "Hey Flavius, why did the chicken cross the Appian Way?" And then Flavius responds, "Don't you ever hear any new jokes?"

Just to be on the safe side, check the library file card system under "Wit and Humor."

Finally, make sure you check for humorous magazines and record albums. In the magazine section, you will find everything from *Mad* through *National Lampoon* to *Punch*. Every library keeps an archive as well, so you may find several back issues to peruse as well as current editions.

In the record section, you will find that most libraries have phonographs and headsets you can check out to sample these albums, or listen to the entire recording if time permits. In fifteen minutes, you can hear some of the best and funniest lines written by the best talent delivered by the top professionals of today, or yesteryear.

Your local library is by far the best and cheapest source of good, usable material. Take some time, browse, ask, and be selective.

Greeting Cards

You read correctly. Greeting cards. Some of the funnier topical material around today is found in the "studio" cards sold in great quantity in supermarkets, pharmacies, and stationery stores. Browse through them, and buy a few for your friends while you're at it. The better greeting card companies use high-quality, current humor and you will probably find more than one idea that's suitable for a jab at old Harry.

Newspapers, Magazines, Etc.

The regular daily and weekly papers and magazines we all read are intended more to inform than amuse, but occasionally you will find the one-liner or offbeat story that will lend itself to the Harry Gordon Roast. Remember that Will Rogers made a whole career out of ". . . just knowing what I read in the papers," and the Johnny Carson evening monologue is full of references to ". . . let's see what was in the papers today."

Be sure to check the movie and theatre reviews for the classic squelch; for example, Dorothy Parker's memorable review of an early Katherine Hepburn performance: "She ran the gamut of emotions from A to B." Would that work in our Roast as: "Harry's bag of career and professional skills covers everything from A to B"?

And last, but not least, don't forget the comics. Some cartoon strips are just visualizations of old jokes that may be rewritten, while others contain current and topical humor that may be relevant as is.

What are the sources of good Roast material? They are as limitless as your imagination. They include networking with friends and associates, radio and television, old joke books, magazines and records, greeting cards, newspapers and magazines, and (oh yes) the one you heard at work just today.

Someone wrote that to a person with a sense of humor, all of life is a comedy. Be alert to it, listen, write it down, revise, and you will be well on your way to developing a library of laughter for Roasts, speeches, and perhaps most important of all, your own personal enjoyment.

WRITING THE FUNNY STORY

In the last chapter, we reviewed the many ways in which to find the funny story, and suggested several useful sources of comedic material. We suggested that there is no such thing as an old joke, as the jokes themselves are ageless, and only a particular joke treatment shows its age.

With our Roast Profile Worksheet and our arsenal of good lines, we have the necessary ingredients to write, tailor, switch, refresh, and personalize the jokes so that, for a moment, our congenial audience may delude itself into thinking that our stories of Harry's unlikely adventures are the gospel truth.

Be sure to give your audience a break and either switch, or get rid of, any jokes that are obviously not appropriate for Harry. In most cases, a switch will solve the problem. Let's say you found this line, you like it and want to use it:

Harry does everything in a first class manner. Last week, for example, I played golf with him and he was using suede golf balls.

Not a bad line, but suppose Harry doesn't play golf and most of his friends know he doesn't? Then a golf line, no matter how intrinsically funny, would fall flat on its figurative face. So, let's see if it can be switched.

As we look at the story again, we can see that our first mistake was in considering it a golf story. It is not. It is a story about Harry's pretenses and concern for appearances which cause him to go to ridiculous lengths in an effort to appear "first class." It just uses the golf metaphor to make its point and is immediately switchable to another sport like tennis (suede tennis balls are also fairly unusual), basketball, squash, etc. Even if Harry is the sedentary indoor type, you might have seen him trying to shoot pool with a suede cue ball. It was only the unlikely and surprising composition of the game ball that made the story funny at all.

If you can't get a line to work for you even after switch-

Or, if Harry had been in the Air Force during World War II, we might go way out on a limb with:

Harry was an accountant in the Air Force during World War II, but he still tells the kids he shot down his share of Zeros.

How did you do? The important point to remember is that no joke should be discarded solely on the basis of age. It can be refreshed, switched, and rewritten. Remember too, that an old joke is new to someone who hasn't heard it before, and in a Roast, the humor often swells from the event itself, which helps give life and appreciation to any honest effort to entertain.

A reasonable question right about here might be: "Where do these writers come from?" Let's address that right now:

Your primary source of writers is the people who want to be in the Roast, followed by the people who will pass in those three-by-five-inch file cards you asked for. You can use them as is, edit, or not use them at all, depending on the quality of the material submitted.

Next, look around the company or organization, and identify the places where writers work. The advertising department is a good bet, as is community/investor/employee/customer relations. Find out who writes your brochures, manuals, customer and vendor correspondence. Go see the wordsmith in the law department or contracts group. You will often find highly talented and creative people in these groups, aching for a chance to write something besides a contractual provision or another good feature of the company's "Super Improved Fractic." Romance them a little with the lights and the fun and the recognition of participating in the Roast. Promise them a mention in the program under the prestigious "Writers, Writers, Writers" section. There are official and unofficial writers hiding all over in any fair-sized organization.

Finally, what about copyrights, stolen material, and

jokes lifted from Johnny Carson and Milton Berle? We were originally going to call this section "Theft Without Guilt" because it may seem that is exactly what we are encouraging you to do. The truth is, as we hope we have proved, that there is no such thing as a new joke—only the treatment can be new. The origin of the joke itself is probably lost somewhere in the deep, dark archives of ancient comedic history. So—when you hear or read the funny story, just identify the comedic element along the lines we have shown you, using Mr. Adams for an example; then refresh it, switch it, stand it on its head, and rewrite it until the story is your own and Harry's.

Now, get out that Roast Profile Worksheet, your stack of jokes, and write yourself a dozen or more good jokes that you could use in tonight's Roast of Harry Gordon.

TELLING THE FUNNY STORY

Excerpt from the telling of a soon-to-be-forgotten story: Somewhere, amidst the wheezing and gasping and uncontrollable laughter, he says: "Oh, I should have told you that it was his brother who wrestled the alligator! The guy who told it to me did a brogue that made the whole thing the funniest story I ever heard . . . I guess you had to be there!"

Some people just can't tell a joke, right? Wrong! Just about anybody can tell a joke if it is right for them, if they become familiar with it, and if they overcome their nervousness through some coaching and rehearsal time. In other words, they can do it if they are willing to work at it.

In fact, some of the best and funniest Roast presenters we have ever seen have been the very people who seemed the least likely to have a funny thing to say. They made the difference by working at it and bringing it off extremely well, with the audience on their side and cheering them on along the way. When we remember that humor is based on surprise and incongruity, then we'll understand that nothing can contribute more to that goal than quiet Mary from Accounting or old Harold from Real Estate coming forth with a well-turned line or two about their good friend Harry.

Let's look at the ingredients of the successful telling and understand what must be done to bring it all together. The starting point is always to:

Select the Material Carefully

There are two sides to this guideline. First, we want to select genuinely funny and topical material as we have discussed elsewhere. Second, we want to carefully select from that yield what suits our particular speaker. Each person would play the role he has laid down for himself in his daily work, his career and his interaction with the audience. Both the speaker and the audience must be comfortable with what the speaker has to say. No one, for example, would accept a story from quiet Mary about the time she and Harry were in the Army together, but they would welcome her story about the time Harry told her he had discovered the secret of living to be 100 years of age:

> "It's simple, Mary," Harry said. "I figure God has an Accounting background, and all you have to do is live to be 51, and hope He rounds up."

In a similar fashion, be wary of asking the wrong person to use any blue material, or indeed any story which is inconsistent with his temperament or his relationship with Harry. Try to let the old folks who have known Harry for years tell the "good old days" stories, and let the younger folks stick to the things that Harry allegedly said or did in more recent times.

It is important to understand that, in assembling your Roasters, you are casting an entertainment and, like any play, you must have the right characters in the right spots.

Be Yourself

You should try to tell your stories and deliver your lines in the same normal way that you would make a verbal report to a group of people in a conference room. Basically, this just means enunciate properly, pronounce each word all the way through as it was written and intended, speak slowly enough to be clearly understood, and loudly enough to be sure everyone can hear you. Maintain good eye contact with your audience as you move back and forth from your notes.

Try the following trick to help, both with the selection of your material, and as an aid to more natural delivery. If you have a favorite comic, it may be that you are attracted by a style which you feel is similar to your own. To see if it works, pick a story that you feel would fit that comic's style, and then try telling it in the way you think that comic would tell it. Try it on tape, and with family or friends, and see what happens. If it sounds good, if it works, you may have found a style that works for you. Keep it and use it for a while. If it doesn't work, discard it but keep the idea of a style to help you in selecting material. If the type of story fits the style, it may be the right kind of story for you, even if you have to tell it in a slightly different way.

You should understand that the audience is on your side. They want you to succeed. They will overlook most minor shortcomings and applaud the smallest triumph. You are among friends.

Rehearse

This point cannot be overemphasized, for without rehearsals, it will not be "okay on the day." The speaker will "die" and might even take the Roast and the rest of the evening along with him. This is tricky ground to cover because you are often dealing with the high-ego person who tells you that he has done a hundred Roasts before, he has always been sensational, he doesn't have time for rehearsals, and he will wing it on the night. You should seriously consider getting such a person off your Roast lineup. He can cause trouble.

We ran another Roast in which the principal Roaster was a well-known corporate executive. At first, it looked too easy. He had agreed to work with us on the script and to rehearse along the way. He kept his bargain, and on the night, appeared on time, rehearsed, and in good order. He took to the microphone like a duck to water and had the whole audience in the palm of his hand within the first few minutes. He was a smash. He did so well, in fact, that his ego took over and he made a big show of ripping up the script, saying "I don't need this," and proceeded to "wing it." From that point on, it was all downhill. Result #1: he was terrible. Result #2: he blamed everyone but himself.

When you plan your rehearsals, make sure to take full advantage of whatever technology is available to you. Start with a cassette recorder and read your material into it in a conversational tone; then play it back and listen to it as objectively as you can. How does it sound? What would you think about that person if you were in the audience? Is it too flat? The right inflection? Too fast or too slow (most people working with a microphone for the first time have a tendency to go very fast)? Play it over again, and this time make a few notes as you listen, on a story-by-story basis if you can. Write out where you need the special emphasis and mark your script or cards accordingly. Then, try it again. Leave the recording overnight and listen to it again over coffee in the morning. How does it sound in the crisp light of day? Work at it until you are satisfied that it represents your best effort. Enlist family and friends to help along the way with constructive criticism and moral support. Tell them you want honesty and objectivity from your "pit team." You will probably get more of it than you bargained for, but that's what you need, so keep asking, keep listening, and keep improving!

If your organization has an audio-visual studio of any sort, hie yourself over there and see if you can arrange for a rehearsal before the cameras. If you can, do it by all means, with this warning: don't let it scare you off!

Any sort of camera is an unforgiving contraption that captures every mole and unbrushed wisp of hair, every false gesture, and every sick-looking smile we can make. It can be a shattering experience to the unprepared. You begin to understand those native tribes who consider cameras as tools of the devil! We know of theatrical people who avoid watching themselves on film or tape because they become too overly critical and find the whole experience too distressing. Given all that, go ahead and do it anyway! The advantages may offset the drawbacks. On videotape you will see the answer to Robbie Burns' prayer about "... would some power the Giftee gie us, to see ourselves as others see us." There we are—live and in color. It is frightening!

After you have played the tape back all the way through once, without reaching for any sharp objects, play it through again, and with the shock out of the way, try to be more objective. Don't get hung up on surface things like whether the clothes clash, or how big your ears are relative to the rest of your head, or how simple you look in those glasses. The audience, who knows you, has discounted that sort of thing years ago, and has accepted you for what you are—big ears and all.

Watch for things like good eye contact and a sense that the person up there is talking to you (with an occasional reference to your notes) and not just reading (with an occasional reference to the audience). If that person is using gestures, decide whether or not they are appropriate and natural. Listen to the person. Is he speaking clearly and loudly enough to be heard? Is he using the microphone well? Some beginners have a tendency to turn their heads while they speak, and so fade in and out of the sound system like this: "... to his uncle, BUT HARRY SAID HE felt we should hit...."

Play it through as many times as you can, try it again if they'll let you, and ask if you can come back again after a few days' rehearsal. Then, for your own peace of mind, say to the technician "Have you ever seen anyone worse?" We'll bet a cup of coffee that you'll get a laugh and an answer that says: "Plenty worse!"

But what if you don't have any of this gear? Then, you should try your talk in front of a full-length mirror. Try a variety of gestures, mug it up and see what works for you.

It's easier to start with exaggerated gestures and tone them down later, than it is to pump life into a dying organism. Keep at it until you feel that the result is acceptable, and then call in the "pit team" for an official opinion.

The Written Notes

Although you should be as familiar as possible with your material, it is not reasonable to expect yourself to memorize it, and it is not smart to try and do it from memory. A memory is a fragile commodity in the best of times ("Harry says there are three signs of old age: short-term memory loss, and he forgets the other two") and in the excitement of the moment you do not want to be standing there with a blank look on your face, as all you can remember is last week's errand list or your short-term position at Silicone Widgets, Inc.

A good bet is to use three-by-five-inch file cards written out, one line per card, with your own personal stage and telling directions. Keep these at hand all evening, take them up to the podium with you, and refer to them as necessary during your Roast presentation. Leave the feats of memory to the professionals (if any) who don't use Teleprompters or some similar memory aid. Just get yourself through the evening's work in as painless and enjoyable a fashion as possible.

The Dry Run

Somehow, get yourself and your group to the scene of the Roast even if it's just a few hours early on the evening of the Roast itself. Try out everything on the scene: lights, microphone, podium, and any other gear you might be using. Stand up there and talk while a friend moves around the hall and reports on how you look and sound. Is there enough light for you to see your notes? Are you talking directly into the microphone, or must you stand back a few inches? Is there any feedback (squeal) in the speakers? If so, turn the system down or at least point the speakers away from the microphone so the system won't "reprocess" the sound. In general, how does everybody sound and look? This last investment of time may pay the richest dividends of all the time you've put in so far.

The secret then is to be yourself, get comfortable with the material and insure it fits you and you it; rehearse in front of the mirror, cassette recorder, video cameras, family and friends. Get your written notes and stage instructions on file cards that you can carry in a pocket and in your hand. Then get yourself to the scene and have a dry run of the whole presentation with a friend who can conduct this final critique of your performance.

Remember that you are staging an entertainment, and your audience is generally friendly. They are out to have a good time and will be rooting for you to succeed along the way.

With a little work on your part, succeed is exactly what you will do.

6

Mechanics
of the Roast

THE ROOM

The type of room you will select for your Roast depends on the type of Roast you are scheduling and the number of people expected. A dinner Roast naturally requires a larger area with set tables and chairs and, most likely, a riser or dais for the Guest of Honor and his Tormentors. A cocktail hour Roast, on the other hand, could most likely be held in a much smaller area with a few folding chairs set up as the Roast hour approaches.

The only hard-and-fast rule you will want to follow in all this is that the room must be private. It must be entirely closed off from the rest of the building, or you will impede the flow of the Roast by making people, who would otherwise make their presentations openly before friends and associates, become "reluctant dragons" in the presence of curious strangers. Get yourself a private room with doors, not curtains, that close. Don't bother other people. Don't let other people bother you.

A word from your Dutch uncle. If you are having a group for dinner, most restaurants will provide a private room at no charge. Some restaurants will do this in smaller rooms for parties as small as ten or twelve. Ask about this at the outset in your discussions with the restaurant management. It is an important ingredient in your final decision.

In general, any good-sized, properly lighted, air conditioned (or heated), attractive room will do. The further from the kitchen, the better. (Food service may be a tad slower, but you'll miss the dropped tray of silverware and the shouted instructions among the kitchen help.) Check on all of these things. Ask for the names of other groups who have used the room for one of their functions, then call their leaders and ask for their opinions.

It is usually desirable to have a head table on the riser at which is seated Harry, the Roast Master, the Principal Tormentors, and their personal guests. The center place at the table should be left open for the portable podium, light, and microphone setup for the speakers' use.

The dinner guests are generally seated eight or ten to a table and, unless you have a lot of time and extraordinary patience, don't get involved with reservations. Let them work that out themselves or have seating on a first come, first served basis.

Make sure you know where all the room controls are located for the heating and cooling, the lights, and the sound system. Try them all yourself to be sure you understand what switch works what. We suggest that you mark each switch with a little piece of masking tape on which you write the switch function. This can easily be removed after the Roast, with no harm done.

Make sure other restaurant guests have no reason to use your private room as a walk-through to restrooms, cloakrooms, parking lots or anything else. The watchword is privacy.

LIGHTS AND SOUNDS

It would be very nice to have some sort of spotlight, or top hat light, shining on the speaker's podium. This should be controlled separately from the main room lights so you can dim the latter without affecting the former. Such a setup may already be in place. Ask about it. If it is not, the restaurant can rig it up for you at little or no cost.

As for the sound system, as we said earlier, it can make or break the evening.

The first thing you do with any sound system is try it out yourself and hear how it sounds. Get someone to hook up a microphone and talk into it while a friend walks around the room and reports on how well you may be heard. Then let the friend talk while you walk and listen. Check the various volume levels until you hear one that sounds just right. Mark that position on the scale with your magic marker and on Roast night, start from that setting and crank up the decibels as necessary to compensate for the audience. Check for feedback, the terrible screeching sound that occurs when the system's speakers are feeding back your sound into the microphone. This can usually be cured by turning the speakers away from the microphone, moving them further apart, or turning down the sound system itself.

Be sure to check any other rooms whose sound systems might play into yours, and vice versa. You do not want your Roast interrupted by music being played in another room, or telephone or reservation pages. Tell the restaurant management that you want a closed sound system that begins and ends in the room you are assigned. Unless they can guarantee you this, visit your local music store or stereo shop and find out about renting a small sound system for the evening. All you really need are a microphone (with podium or on stand), an amplifier, and some speakers. It's usually not much money and can save you a lot of aggravation on the night. It is no coincidence, we have learned, that professional entertainers go to the great effort and expense of carrying whole busloads of sound equipment around with them. You cannot enjoy what you cannot hear.

Before we leave lights and sound, a few words on the podium itself. A podium serves several useful purposes, like giving inexperienced speakers something to stand behind and hold onto. Also, on its slanted front, you can lay out your notes for quick and easy reference. It holds the microphone firmly in position so that a nervous speaker whose hands are shaking doesn't even have to try.

The podium should have a light for your notes, and that

light should be separate from all other lights so that when the room is darkened, the podium light remains bright enough to read by. You might even consider having a one- or two-step stand in back so shorter speakers can tower over the podium just as their taller colleagues do.

If the room is set up and the temperature comfortable, and you feel in command of lights and sound, you are ready to consider the most important step of all—guest safety.

GUEST SAFETY

You would be amazed at the number of times careless hotel and restaurant people have failed to properly mark fire exits, or have done something incredibly stupid like locking exit doors with deadbolts or piling storage in front of them. One has only to read the papers, unfortunately, to see several examples of this needless waste of life each year.

During your first visit to the property, ask about the fire exits and walk through each and every one of them right up to, and including, opening the outside door. Check for fire extinguishers along the way, and check the inspection dates on the tags. If they are not recent, it indicates a lack of management concern for its patrons, and should be reported. Remember that as Roast Master, the safety of the guests is your responsibility as surely as if they were guests in your home.

While you're checking, check the emergency lights. Those are the battery-powered flood lights usually found mounted somewhere along the room's wall. They are supposed to go on (using their batteries) when the main power fails. Try them out. They all have test buttons on the front panel, which interrupts house current so you can prove that the batteries work. When you push the test buttons, the lights must come on. Otherwise, report them. Also, make sure these lights cover the room, the hallway to a nearby exit, restrooms, etc., so no one will be stuck in the dark, should there be a power failure.

If all is well, and in a reputable restaurant it should be, just make a few notes and explain all of this at the beginning of the Roast, under the Roast Master's administrative notes. You might consider something like this:

> Good Evening, ladies and gentlemen, and welcome to the Harry Gordon Roast. Before we begin the evening's proceedings, I have a few housekeeping notes. First of all, the exits are there and there, etc., etc., second, a few notes on food service, payment, or whatever . . . and now. . . .

For those who think the topic grim, let us suggest that the alternative would be even more grim if people did not know, and needed to. Just treat the matter of safety as important, but routine, just as airline personnel do when they start telling you about oxygen, vests, life rafts, and the like. None of this, to our knowledge, has frightened anyone off an airplane yet.

FOOD SERVICE

If you are going to offer a dinner, make it a good one. This does not mean it has to be expensive; just well prepared. Not every chicken has to be a rubber chicken and the main difference is in preparation, the quality of the kitchen, and timing. You should check the food service during an early visit, and the best way to do that is to eat there. Select the sorts of dishes you might have at the Roast, and see how they are done. Remember as you dine that you are evaluating the food, its preparation, and the restaurant service. All must be done professionally.

We often ask to see the kitchen. It keeps the restaurant honest even if you don't know exactly what you're looking for. Beware of the staff that isn't proud to display its food preparation areas. As you walk through the kitchen, make sure, at least, that it is clean and that the people who work in it are clean. It is one thing to be spotted by the soup of the day; it is quite another to be dirty. The best way to evaluate a kitchen is to ask yourself this question: now, having seen the kitchen, would I want to eat here again? If the answer is yes, you are on target.

A restaurant has only two ways to make money: raise the prices or lower the costs. Sit down with the restaurant management and find out exactly what you are getting. Will there be cloth or paper tablecloths and napkins? Will they use only china, or might dessert appear on paper plates? Will the glasses be glasses, or plastic? Find out. If these things don't mean much to you, maybe you can trade them off for something you do want—like matchbooks on each table commemorating Harry and his Roast. The most anyone can say is "no," and you won't get anything unless you ask for it.

Having done all this, remember that the timing of the dinner is your responsibility too. If you tell the restaurant that dinner should be served at eight, they will probably be ready. You had better be ready too or your "fashionably lates" will turn your prime rib into leather. Tell your guests that dinner is scheduled fifteen minutes earlier than it really is, and that there are no refunds. Motivation helps.

The mechanics of the Roast are probably the most straightforward part of the whole event. They respond to checklists, work, and follow-up with very little human intervention. If you have chosen a good property and work with them openly and honestly, they can help you enormously.

Just be sure to walk the floor and check everything on two occasions: during the selection process, and early on the evening of the Roast. You want correct preparation, equipment readiness, and safety.

THE BLACK BAG

Every Roast Master needs a little black bag (color is optional) containing items that may be needed and may not be available on the night. Here's what we carry:

1. A good sturdy flashlight with fresh batteries and bulb, and replacements for both.

2. An extension cord, an adaptor that makes one electrical outlet into two or three (clear this first with
   the restaurant management to guard against fire
   hazard), and a 3:2 plug adaptor or two so your three-
   prong stereo plug can fit into their two-hole electrical
   outlet.

3. Tools, such as a plain and Phillips head screwdriver
   set and insulated side cutter pliers.

4. Electrical tape, masking tape, and marking pens.

5. A spare bulb and fuse for the podium and any other
   electrical gear you provide.

6. Pen and paper for notes.

Got it all in good order? Then—on to the Roast!

7

The Master
of Ceremonies:
The Roast Master

The Master of Ceremonies (MC), or Roast Master (RM), is the Captain of the Roast Event. He is the man on the field, calling the plays, and generally making sure that everything goes in accordance with the plan. It is the most visible and most important of the Roast jobs and, if you want to retain full control, a job you should keep for yourself. If you cannot or will not do that, then you must get out of the way and let the RM do his job within the parameters and guidelines set forth in the Roast Profile Worksheet, or as may be suggested by the Guest of Honor, the audience, the location, or the Roast vehicle itself.

Throughout this book, we have stressed the necessity of preparation and rehearsal, and the Roast Master is the person who must carry it all out. He will work with the presenters from material selection through rehearsal, constructively critiquing, assisting, cajoling, and otherwise gently reinforcing his role as the Master of the Roast.

The RM has many jobs during the preparation stages, but it is on the night of the Roast that he comes fully into his own. Here are some of the things he will be expected to do.

The Roast Master will call the Roast to order and deal with any safety, administrative, or housekeeping notes as may be appropriate. He will state the purpose of the evening's entertainment, and introduce the guest of honor and other guests both on and off the dais. He will introduce and call the speakers, assisting them on and off as necessary. He will handle transitions and aid the smooth flow of the

Roast from speaker to speaker. He will present such awards as are scheduled, and conclude with a final wrap-up thanking all for their assistance in making the Roast event successful.

To accomplish all this, the Roast Master needs a lot of material which should be written out and rehearsed just as for any other speaker. He will need as many introductions and transitions as he has speakers, as well as a few extra, should any speakers come up short. If awards are in order, he should have such a talk available suitable to the guest, the audience, and the award itself.

He probably should have a few "anti-heckler" lines in his back pocket as well, in the event of an onslaught that he does not choose to ignore or let the audience handle. A friendly audience that wants the evening to proceed in proper order, can and will police itself.

The RM's biggest problem will probably be the friendly speaker who, once on, can't get off. It is one of the oddities of public speaking but it invariably happens.

Good old Charlie has a script and has rehearsed, wants to contribute, is an obliging fellow in every sense of the word, but, when he stands in front of the lights, in front of the microphone, with that friendly and captive crowd before him—something snaps. I don't know what it is. Some say it is the thrill of power (". . . all those people, and they must listen to me!") but whatever it may be, Charlie falls victim to the illness that has plagued speeches, lectures, sermons, homilies, and talks of every sort since the beginning of time: long windedness. Thus, we have the Two Great Truths of Public Speaking:

1. People who don't have much to say take a very long time to say it.
2. A fool and his microphone are soon connected.

The Roast Master must control this sort of person and there are several ways to do it.

1. Tell everyone at the outset that you are concerned about this phenomenon and will not permit it. Tell them that you will signal an overlong speaker, give a minute or two for a final wrap-up, and then react as necessary.

2. An early reaction might be a barb line or two in the spirit of the Roast:

"Charlie, they are checking their watches out there . . . no, that guy's marking a calendar."

"You have just heard that famous Chinese philosopher and speaker, 'On Too Long' ."

3. Have a buzzer, bell, or some other noisemaker at hand. Use it and loudly announce a "Two Minute Warning," then walk to the microphone and gently assist in the speaker wrap-up.

The windbag can be a mortal enemy of the Roast. Let him save face, but control or silence him before he does the evening in.

The Roast Master has a big job as speaker, host, entertainer, and enforcer. Like the pilot of a plane, he must be in command of the Roast event regardless of whatever more exalted ranks may be present on or off the dais. Make that perfectly clear to everybody at the outset of the Roast event.

8

Tonight's the Night: A Harry Gordon Roast Script

What follows now is a segment from the Harry Gordon Roast in which we bring together in practice what we have been preaching all through the book.

Our imaginary Roast Master, whom we pick up in mid-Roast, will introduce the last three Tormentors, and then Harry himself.

First we will hear from Bill, who works for Harry. He will be followed by Ed, a business associate and personal friend, and then by Arthur, who is Harry's boss.

Last, but certainly not least, we will hear from the man, Harry Gordon, the guest of honor.

Relax now, sit back, and try to visualize the setting. It is after dinner, and everyone is comfortable and in good spirits. The Roast has gone very well so far, and everybody, including Harry, seems to be enjoying himself.

Shhhh. The Roast Master is speaking:

Roast Master: . . . *And now, ladies and gentlemen, we will hear from the man who has worked for Harry these past five years.*

We thought it only appropriate that Harry should meet a couple of his employees before he left, so join me now in welcoming . . . Bill!

Bill: *Thank you, ladies and gentlemen, for inviting me here tonight to speak of my friend, my boss, and my mentor —Harry Gordon. Which one is he?*

Just kidding, Harry. I hope that's a smile.

Perhaps only a few times in each lifetime do we get a chance to honor a man of great intelligence, wit, and wisdom. Unfortunately, this is not one of those times.

Tonight, we honor Harry Gordon, your friend and colleague, and my boss.

When I agreed to speak tonight, our Roast Master said I must come to his office and select one of the approved topics for tonight's program. Well, I got there late and most of the good ones were already taken. In fact, there were only three left, and I took all three so you could participate in my selection process:

The speaker produces three file cards which he proceeds to read, one at a time, as follows:

The first topic was "Harry Gordon, a manager for the Eighties" (pause, then rip up paper).

The second topic was "Harry Gordon, the Professional's Professional" (pause, then rip up paper).

And the third topic, which I finally selected, was "Harry Gordon, the Man and his Music."

Harry's watching me out of the corner of his eye. Don't worry, Harry, I'm not going to say anything bad about you. Like most people who work for you, our relationship is based on more than just trust and respect; our relationship is based on fear.

There are a lot of people in your group who believe in you, Harry—but there are a lot of people in your group who believe in the easter bunny too.

I'm going to talk about Harry Gordon, the Renaissance Man. We call him that because most of his thinking seems to come from the fifteenth century.

But he is a man of many interests. He plays the violin, for example. How many knew that? He used to play in all the local vaudeville shows, but he quit when they kept putting him on after the monkey act and people thought he was just an encore.

It was only recently that he gave up his dreams of be-

coming a concert violinist—after several death threats were received on Boston Pops stationery.

Harry confided in me once that he never really liked playing the violin anyway. Unless he held it perfectly level, his drink kept sliding off.

When Harry quit music, he decided to take on the field of literature. Literature surrendered shortly after.

Such insights the man has! It was he who summed up Shakespeare this way: "Just a bunch of old quotes strung together."

So Harry became a writer, but not without suffering a few setbacks first.

One publisher said they had to rewrite his stuff before they threw it away.

Another rejected not only what he sent in, but anything he might write in the future.

Then—paydirt! He published that engineering book which made the best seller list—in his family.

But he's still the same unspoiled guy he always was. He told me just tonight that he had been offered a contract by the Book-of-the-Month Club. I said, "That's great, Harry, did you take it?" He said, "No, I could never write a book a month."

We know, Harry, we know.

We know what it's like to work for a guy who complains so much, that tonight, after dinner, the head waiter came over and said, "Sir, was anything all right?"

We know what your secretary means when she says things like: "Mr. Gordon, next week is Thanksgiving—if that's all right with you."

We know what it's like to work for a boss who lets you run your own show—as long as he writes the script and directs.

But in your defense, Harry, we know that we haven't seen all of your management skills and techniques. Company policy expressly forbids beatings.

And so, Harry, we all honor you tonight on your retire-

ment. How ironic it is that after all these years the personnel department finally got you to take one of their aptitude tests—only to learn that you were best suited for retirement all along.

Look at the crowd that showed up tonight to honor you on your forthcoming retirement. Who was it who said: "Give the public what they want and they'll come out in droves"?

And we'll remember you Harry, through the little motto which, even as we speak, is being chiseled into the door of your office. It reads "Harry Gordon: He gave us a lot of trouble. It was all he ever gave us."

Thank you all, and good luck, Harry!

Roast Master: *Thank you Bill, that was really well done. It takes a lot of guts to roast the boss like that. No judgment at all, but a whole lot of guts.*

Next, Harry, we have a personal friend of yours on the agenda. Well, you said to dig up somebody from the old days, and it looks like that's where we got him.

Join us, Harry, in welcoming your friend, Ed!

Ed: *Thank you, Roast Master, everyone. Good evening, Harry! I'm here to tell them about the old days, okay?*

The years have been kind to you, Harry. But the weeks in between really knocked the hell out of you.

Well, in his younger days, Harry was an example to us all. He didn't smoke, drink, run around; and there was never any evidence that he ever tried any mind-expanding drugs.

He was an old world sort of guy. Might remind you of an old kerosene lamp—not especially bright; smoked; was often turned down; burned out a few times; and ran out of fuel just when you needed him.

I see some of you taking notes. I don't want these stories about Harry broadcast all over the organization. They were told to me in confidence, and I'm telling them to you in confidence.

Your Roast Master asked me to tell about Harry's days in uniform. I told him if you've heard one Boy Scout story, you've heard them all.

But, okay, let's go back in time a bit, and see how a man like Harry gets started in life. Better yet, what has to go wrong to produce a Harry Gordon?

Now, you've probably all heard stories about Harry's old, old family. He once showed me his family history for 1492, the year Columbus discovered America! It was marked "Volume Six."

Anyway, through the many weaknesses of the Indian immigration laws, the Gordon family got a foothold in the new world.

Then, according to the family Bible, the family went west in a covered wagon. I saw some old family pictures in that Bible and I fully understand why that wagon had to be covered.

Harry talks about his great, great granduncle, Jubal Gordon, who, he says, was elevated by the ranchers to a position of great height. That's one way to say they strung him up.

Harry says Jubal was a precognitive equestrian detective. That means he found horses that nobody knew were lost.

And so, the Gordon family moved on to Texas, where Harry was born during the Great Depression. Not the country's—his father's.

And Harry? How did all of this history affect his formative years? We know, for example, that when he was ten years old, his family very nearly lost him. His father wrote at the time: "I should have taken him further into the hills."

His dad also wrote about the time a rattlesnake bit Harry on the leg during a camping trip. How horrible it must have been, watching the rattler twitch and die!

But Harry never looked back! He went on to school! First to the University of Texas for an engineering degree (that's what they give the guys who couldn't make the team) and then on to Harvard for an MBA. A good plan!

The family hoped for a Harvard education and Aggie smarts. Once again, Harry proved himself master of his own destiny; he came away with an Aggie education—and Harvard smarts.

During this time, there was an "incident" which the family managed to hush up. Two beautiful young women fought a duel over Harry to see which of them would get him. They both got him. One got him in the arm; the other got him in the leg.

But wounds heal, and Harry began his meteoric career rise up to—the middle.

Harry claims his first job was as a diamond cutter. This is technically true. He mowed the lawn on a ball field.

Then, big business beckoned, and Harry went to work for the Hanes underwear company where he was widely known as "Inspector 13."

But nothing is forever. The military called. The peace had been broken. In a sneak dawn attack, Fort Sumter had been fired upon. Sorry, Harry! I mean Pearl Harbor was attacked, and within several days Harry was in the Army.

Harry, these notes aren't clear. Which Army was that? Ours? And we won?

Harry doesn't like to talk about the war years; even the parts that he remembers. Let's just say he fought his way through every tight scrape from Texas to California and then—it was over! Harry came east to work for West Design Labs.

Harry let everbody know right at the outset that he was nobody's "yes man." When the boss said "no," Harry said "no" too.

And he worked to improve himself. He took a speed reading course, for example. He read the entire Bible in just under twenty minutes—said it had something to do with God.

And the rest is history; right, Harry? You brought new meaning to the phrase: "With age comes wisdom, but sometimes age comes alone."

Or this phrase "Some are born to greatness, others have greatness thrust upon them." A few, like Harry, duck.

But that's enough from me, Harry, I know how it is. You finally get it all together—and then you forget where you left it.

So I'll leave you with this toast: "Here's to the world,

the merry old world, and the days, be they gray or blue. And here's to the fates, may they bring what they may, and the best of them all: Here's to you!"

Thank you.

Roast Master: *Thank you, Ed. People say that you are outspoken, but I don't know by whom.*

And now, we will hear from a man who probably deserves the croix de guerre or, as Harry would say, "At least he deserves a medal."

Ladies and Gentlemen, please welcome Harry's Boss— Arthur!

Arthur: *Thank you all very much.*

Ladies and gentlemen, distinguished members of the dais, good old what's-your-name, (sorry) Harry.

What can you say about a man who came from humble beginnings and rose to the very heights of industry based solely on intelligence, grit, and the will to push on where others might fall back? A man who has so distinguished himself among his peers that no right-thinking person can say a word against him? Well, enough about me; we're here to talk about Harry Gordon.

What can I say about Harry? He's been called cold, rude, self-centered, arrogant, and egotistical. But that's just his family's opinion.

He never did me any harm, and I've always believed that what doesn't kill you outright strengthens you in the long run.

Well, I'm the guy who has been riding the tiger all these years. I hesitate to call myself Harry's boss because Harry never accepted that premise; so there's probably no reason that you should.

Harry just looked at me and said, "You're my boss?" Up to now he thought I was unlisted.

What's it like having a guy like Harry working for you? Well, I named my first ulcer after him.

We like to think of our staff as a championship football

team. *(Name) is the halfback, (name) is the fullback, I'm the quarterback, and Harry's the drawback.*

Why did we hire him, you ask? Well, he came highly recommended. He had marvelous letters of reference from his previous employers, Larry, Moe, and Curly.

He quickly proved himself to be a salesman at heart. Once I saw him add 20 and 20 and get 100. I asked, "Where did the other 60 come from?" He said, "That's next year's potential."

And pushy? Harry's always after that extra inch. Once he was at my house for a party ("once" is about right too) and I introduced him to a doctor friend of mine. Harry embarrassed us all by telling the guy his symptoms. My friend finally had to say "Look, I'm not an M.D., I'm a Doctor of Philosophy!" Harry thought about that for ten seconds and then said, "Okay then, what is the meaning of life?"

And aggressive? This morning, the receptionist said, "Have a nice day," and Harry said, "Don't tell me what to do."

And cheap? Did you see him after dinner tonight? I don't mind a guy who takes home doggie bags, but he's got plastic wrap in his pockets for the soup!

And egocentric? At the last meeting of the Engineering Society, Harry introduced a prominent colleague as "the second best engineer in the world." I said, "That's terrible, Harry. You go apologize to that man." So Harry walks over to him and says, "I'm sorry you're the second best engineer in the world."

Well, enough of his finer points.

Anyway, Harry says that he always profits from his mistakes. If that's true, Harry, you are on the edge of one helluva banner year!

But, relative to our company, we all know the kind of impact Harry has made. You can, right now, call any of our plants and offices throughout North America and talk to whoever answers the phone, mention Harry Gordon's name, and they will all say the same thing: "Who the hell is Harry Gordon?"

Thank you and goodnight.

Roast Master: *Thank you, Arthur, for that beautiful sentiment. Wonderfully restrained, I might add.*

Well, what about it, ladies and gentlemen? Shall we keep the fun going, or should we listen to Harry?

You are right, you are right. He sat through it all in proper order so it is about time we gave him his say.

Ladies and gentlemen, your attention then is directed to the podium where our very own worm is about to turn.

I give you our guest of honor—Mr. Harry Gordon!

Harry Gordon: *Thank you, thank you all very much. It's a great pleasure to be among friends, even if they're not my friends.*

I'll be brief. I'm sure you are all anxious to get home to your "I Love Lucy" reruns.

Did you all notice with me that, counting the Roast Master, there are seven speakers on the dais tonight? I spent the whole evening waiting for Snow White to show up.

It's probably just as well she didn't. Nobody in a white dress would stand a chance against that bunch.

Seriously though, I will have to admit that this has been one of the most exciting and enjoyable evenings of my life—if I discount everything that has happened up until now.

And to think I cancelled a dentist's appointment to be here.

Perhaps it's just culture shock; back in Texas we say eulogies over our dead. Up here, apparently, the dead do their own talking.

First of all, I would like to thank the Roast Master and the committee who brought us all together and made this evening happen. Those of us who felt you couldn't organize a two-float parade were obviously wrong.

I enjoyed your little introductions and commentaries as well. Frankly, I would have enjoyed them more, had you given me a better seat. The one I had faced you.

Bill, I really enjoyed your little talk. It was up to your usual substandard.

Being your boss wasn't all that easy either. I was never trained in the remedial arts.

Stay there a moment more. I want to remember you just the way you were tonight—employed.

Ed, you did a good job, too.

Ed told you about my military career because he never had one of his own. He was one of the angry young men of the 1960s. He played frisbee for peace.

Ed's our treasurer, as you know. The treasurer is usually an accountant with table manners and his own suit. One out of two isn't bad, Ed.

Did you all know I helped train Ed? That's right. When he came here, he thought margins were those little black lines you had to stay inside of when you color.

Oh, look over there. Did you see that? Bill was nodding off again. A late one, eh, Bill? Normally, I only see Bill during working hours, and it never occurred to me that he must sleep at night, too.

And Arthur, what can I say about you?

Linguists tell us there are 25,000 useless words in the English language, and you hit every damn one of them tonight.

Your little talks are always refreshing. People feel so much better after a nap.

Arthur can take credit for a lot of things, but he's always willing to share a little with the person who actually did it.

The first time I saw Arthur, I said, "Someday, that man will be our president." Of course, the first time I saw Liz Taylor, I said, "Someday, she'll be a nun."

What was it like working for Arthur? Put it this way: making a mistake in front of Arthur was like cutting yourself in front of Dracula.

Dracula may have been more tolerant.

And as for all of you, my friends, who came out to be with me tonight, I saved the very best for you.

First, you have my thanks and my love.

Then, I'll leave you with a toast: May we never crack a joke that scratches our friendship; may we always be happy, and our enemies know it; and may we all have the "four L's" of Life: Length of days, Loyalty, Laughter, and Love.

Thank you, and goodnight.

Roast Master: *Harry Gordon, everyone!*

9

Best Roast Lines: A Comprehensive Compendium of Cutting Comments and Comic Characterizations

These are the jokes, folks.

They are the best new treatments of the comedic elements found in the six basic types of jokes that we identified and discussed in an earlier chapter. With these stories to draw upon, you now have all the ingredients of the successful social or business Roast.

We have tied the jokes to the Roast Profile Worksheet in the order in which you will require them. That order is as follows:

I.   Introductions

II.   The Roast Profile Worksheet

III.   Assaults and Zappers

IV.   Segués and Transitions

V.   Wrap-Ups and Toasts

VI.   For Women Only

VII.   For the Hecklers

Let's review each of these major categories in a little more detail

I. Introductions: Most of these are Roast Master lines to be used for introducing guest speakers as well as the guest of honor. If you have to introduce anyone, look here for ideas.

II. Roast Profile Worksheet Lines: Here are lines tied to the 16 numbered paragraphs of the Roast Profile Worksheet.

Item 9 of the Roast Profile Worksheet, for example, asks

about Harry's service background; so, in paragraph 9 of this section, you will find all the service-related jokes you will need for the Roast.

III. Assaults and Zappers: These are Roast lines more general in nature, that you may want to plug in as the mood suits you or as you need more general, or filler, material.

Once the Roast is written with as many relevant lines as possible, you may look here for whatever you need to flesh it out.

IV. Segués and Transitions: Again, these are mostly for the Roast Master's use in getting speakers on and off the program. From these, you may select the patter that keeps the program moving forward as you work your way through your speakers to the guest of honor and the wrap-up.

V. Wrap-Ups and Toasts: Everyone needs a close, a way to get off, and you'll find some good ideas here. Whether you are Roast Master or speaker, you'll find a closing line or toast in this section.

VI. For Women Only: Most of the jokes about Harry can easily be rewritten, or refreshed, along the lines we have discussed, to cover the situation where Harry turns out to be Harriet. Here are a few traditional jokes to help out along the way.

VII. For the Hecklers: The audience should not be a problem in a business/social Roast situation, but occasionally it is. Here are a few ways to encourage them to keep their comments to their innermost selves.

And—that's it! Be sure to read all the joke sections as your time permits. What we felt was relevant in one category, you may find fits several, as far as your Harry (or Harriet) is concerned.

Good Luck—and Happy Roasting!

I. INTRODUCTIONS

1. Here he is, the Man of the Week . . . shows you what kind of a week it has been.

2. Usually, we roast guys we love, admire, and respect. Tonight is an exception.

3. Harry is a manager who successfully defied the Industrial Revolution.

4. I was responsible for bringing together all the people who love and respect him. They're waiting outside in the phone booth.

5. If conceit is God's gift to little people, he is truly blessed.

6. Here he is: living proof that you don't have to break a mirror to have seven years of bad luck . . .

7. Here he is now, the Marquis de suede . . .

8. They told me to say something nice about Harry. Well, he doesn't shed.

9. You and I go back a long time Harry, and I don't deserve the support you've given me over the years. But then, I'm losing my hair, and I don't deserve that either.

10. By the time I got to pick a subject for tonight, there were only three left:

    A. Harry Gordon: "A Manager For All Ages" (Pause-Rip Up)

    B. Harry Gordon: "The Warm Human Being" (Pause-Rip Up)

    . . . and the one I finally chose . . .

    C. Harry Gordon: "The Man And His Music."

11. He had a redeeming social grace once, but he sold it.

12. Here's a man who's taken a lot of abuse, and rightly so.

13. I'm glad this isn't a Catholic dinner. The last time I went to a Catholic dinner, I left my car at the curb and it was raffled off.

14. But success hasn't changed him. He's still the same arrogant bastard he always was.

15. Harry claims to be a self-made man—I think it's damn nice of him to take the blame.

16. Harry's an old world sort of guy . . . might remind you of a kerosene lamp: he's not especially bright, smokes a lot, is often turned down, and tends to go out just when you need him most.

17. They say that there are twenty-five thousand useless words in the English language. You are now about to hear most of them.

18. First a warning: I don't want these Harry stories broadcast all over the company. I'm telling them to you in confidence because they were told to me in confidence.

19. It looks like everyone is really enjoying this evening together. Shall we keep the fun going for a while yet, or shall I introduce Harry?

20. Thackeray said that beauty was a lease which one is compelled to resign after forty years. Tonight, we see yet another instance of an early retirement.

21. I hope you all know that we wouldn't say anything about Harry unless it was good. Well, what you're going to hear tonight is really good!

22. I have spoken about many men and women in my time, and tonight I will speak about Harry. In Economics that's known as the Law of Diminishing Returns.

23. You know it's a tribute to this man that he has made such an impact that you can go anywhere in the country—East Coast, West Coast, North or South—and ask anyone about Harry and they'll all say the same thing. (pause) Who the hell is Harry Gordon?

24. Say what you will, there's only one Harry Gordon. (pause) I found that out by looking in the telephone directory.

25. And here to spread a little dullness . . .

26. Speaking of things that aren't as they used to be, here's Harry Gordon!

27. Here he is now, the author of "Ten Ways To Roast A Turkey."

28. Harry, we don't want you to come up here and tell us that you're unworthy of friends like us. We already know that.

29. Harry Gordon: "A Legend in His Own Mind."

30. When Harry heard he was going to speak tonight, he asked me how to come across as a warm, sensitive, and witty person. So I helped him select and hire a double.

31. And here he is now, Lawrence Welk's long lost son, the human dynamo himself, the man who yawns in the face of danger (and every other face for that matter) . . .

32. What can I say about him . . . that he hasn't already said himself?

33. Once or twice in a career you get a chance to introduce somebody who's at the top of his trade. A person whose name is synonymous with competence, integrity, enthusiasm. Unfortunately, this is not one of those times.

34. Will Rogers said that every man is ignorant, just on different subjects. Let me introduce the most multi-subject ignorant guy I know.

35. Tonight my job is to talk and your job is to listen. Let me know if you finish up before I do.

36. Here he is now, a six-time award loser.

37. Harry was very nervous when we told him he had to speak tonight. He said: "What if they boo me?" We told him: "Harry, they can't boo and yawn at the same time."

38. Before I introduce Harry tonight, I'd like to make a comment of my own: in any list of the Fashionable 400, the man you are about to hear would certainly be one of the zeros.

39. We had one major disappointment tonight: (popular name) couldn't make it . . . and Harry could.

40. Will Rogers said, "I never met a man I didn't like." Will

Rogers was gone many years before our next speaker was born.

41. Here's a man who always uses his head. He knows it's the little things that count.

42. We like to think of ourselves as a championship football team. (Name) is the quarterback, (name) the halfback, and (name) the fullback. Now I'd like to introduce Harry, our drawback.

43. Here he is, our very own man of the world (who is getting bigger and bigger around the equator): Harry Gordon)

44. Here he is, our very own aphid in the rose bush of life: Harry Gordon!

45. They say there are three kinds of people in every organization: rowboats, sailboats, and steamboats. The rowboat people move only when pushed and shoved, the sailboat people move, but only when the wind is right, and the steamboat people just churn along on their own, day and night, good weather and bad. I'd like you to welcome our very own steamboat: Harry Gordon!

46. I discovered Harry Gordon. I discovered him once in a broom closet, once in the janitor's room, and once in the rear parking lot . . .

47. Here he is now, living proof of the old saw that you put optimists in (Sales) and pessimists in (Finance) . . .

48. (Toast) Here's to my friends, wise and otherwise.

49. Here he is, then, the man who sticks the match of enthusiasm to the fuse of energy, and then just naturally explodes . . . Harry Gordon!

50. Okay, I think I'll introduce Harry now; I can stand surprise better than I can stand suspense.

51. Here he is now, the only bull who owns his own china shop . . .

52. Here he is now, the world's shortest giant . . .

53. Here he is now, the world's tallest midget . . .

54. On our list of organizational movers and shakers, I'd like to introduce our chief twitch.

55. And now it is a pleasure to introduce—your favorite and his—Harry Gordon!

56. Harry Gordon: a man who did a lot for American Industry . . . but why did it all have to be for our company?

57. Here he is now, the latest dope on Wall Street: Harry Gordon!

58. You have heard of the "One Minute Manager," and the "One Minute Parent" . . . now I'd like to introduce the "One Minute Lover," Harry Gordon!

59. Presenting . . . our Premier Postprandial Presenter, Provocateur of Puns, Perpetrator of Persiflage, and Panjandrum of Peppy Patter: Harry Gordon!

60. And now, let's hear from the female of the speeches. . .

61. Some people are young and some people are old, and a very few are just young for a very long time. Please welcome: Harry Gordon!

62. And now, a man who single-handedly disproves Darwin's Survival of the Fittest Theory: Harry Gordon!

63. And now, we're going to hear from (name), our corporate wordsmith. When he's through, we'll pass among you with the English Language Version of his talk.

64. Where there's smoke, there's Harry!

II. ROAST PROFILE WORKSHEET

4. Age

1. He's a mature business thinker . . . all his ideas are fifty years old.

2. He told me the secret of living to be one hundred: get past fifty and hope that God rounds up.

3. He's not really a confirmed old bachelor. He'll probably get married at seventy and look for a house near a school.

4. During the war years he once got a letter of appreciation from Roosevelt. That was very nice of Teddy.

5. You can tell a Texan's age by counting the sweat rings in his hat.

6. Is he a talker? He wore out two pairs of lips before he was twenty.

7. Harry: you get one hundred life points for carrying on a twenty-five year love affair . . . unassisted.

8. We tried to dig up someone who knew Harry when he was young; and "dig them up" is about what we'd have to do.

9. He got an award from the President; one of the few Lincoln gave out.

10. He's working his way through the three ages of hair: parted, unparted, departed.

11. When we were planning tonight's dinner, I went down into the wine cellar and we found something tucked away in the corner, over fifty years old, and covered with dust. It was Harry.

12. He looks the same as he did ten years ago, but, so does a dollar bill.

13. Harry says he just turned forty. It must have been a U-turn.

14. Some people on the committee tried to count the candles on his cake, but they were driven back by the heat.

15. They say that Wisdom comes with Age, Harry, but I guess sometimes Age just comes alone.

16. In his youth Harry loved wine, women, and song. He can still sing.

17. Harry told me the other day that there are two ways to tell if you're getting old. The first is loss of memory. He couldn't think of the other one.

18. Harry says the two signs of advancing age are when everything hurts . . . and what doesn't hurt, doesn't work.

19. Did you know Harry was a War Baby? His parents took one look at him and started fighting.

20. It's a shame that when Harry has finally learned to make the most of life, most of it is gone.

21. I would like to repeat to Harry what a wise old man once said to me. If you want to live to be a hundred, first you've got to make it to ninety-nine and then the last year—take it easy.

22. His family finally got Harry to go in for a medical check-up. He said "What could be wrong with me? I have a cast-iron stomach, nerves like steel bands, and a will of iron!" Well, they found rust.

23. Well Harry, at least the "Battle of the Sexes" isn't your worry anymore.

24. It's just not fair, Harry. Whatever Mother Nature gave you, Father Time has taken away.

25. Harry's at that difficult age where he's too old to work and too poor to retire.

26. Harry's at the age where he doesn't have to worry about avoiding temptation. Temptation avoids him.

27. I don't know exactly how old he is but he was circumcised with a stone knife.

28. He's so old that his social security number is two digits.

29. He thinks young. One day he said to one of the secretaries "I hate to think of life at the age of forty-five." She said, "Why, what happened to you then?"

30. He took me to a Gay Nineties bar. The few guys there who weren't gay were over ninety.

31. Harry's a man of some forty summers . . . and half again that many winters.

32. Harry's found the secret of eternal youth. He lies about his age.

33. I knew Harry was getting old when I peeked into his

little black book one day . . . and saw all the names and numbers were doctors.

34. Harry, just remember that there are many, many advantages to old age (long pause) . . . I was just trying to think of some.

35. Harry is a man who combines the wisdom of youth with the energy of old age.

36. I don't want to suggest that Harry married a bit late in life . . . but Medicare picked up 75 percent of the honeymoon.

37. Harry, just look at your age this way: if you were a redwood tree, you wouldn't even be through puberty yet.

38. I went to a party at Harry's once, but all of his friends seemed so old. Every time I set down my glass, someone was putting their teeth in it.

39. One good thing about growing old, Harry, you don't have to go camping.

40. Harry had a lot of charisma in his early years, but lately it cleared up.

41. You know, Harry, there are a lot of advantages to growing old. It's just that we can never think of them.

42. I told Harry he shouldn't go out with young girls. He asked "Why? I can do them no harm, they get a fine dinner out of it, and I always make sure their homework is done."

43. The only vice he can still handle is the one on his workshop bench.

44. Harry's at that age when the iron in his blood turns to lead, and settles in his behind.

45. A fortuneteller once told him that he'd be poor, out of shape, and dissatisfied until he reached the age of forty. "What then?" Harry asked. "Then," said the fortuneteller, "you'll get used to it."

46. Harry has no respect for age, unless it is bottled.

47. Harry has been around a long time. Just twenty-five years ago he used to dream of earning the salary he's starving on today.

48. Harry and his wife celebrated their twentieth anniversary with a second honeymoon; went back to the hotel, got the same room, and he sent out for hors d'oeuvres, champagne, and oxygen.

49. How old is Harry? He won't say exactly, but he admits loaning Alexander Graham Bell a nickel to make the first phone call. Probably got repaid in stock too.

50. The doctor told him: "I can't make you any younger!" Harry said, "Just make sure I grow older."

51. Harry's at the awkward age: young enough to smile at a pretty girl, but too old for her to smile back.

52. We've got some people here tonight who went to school with you, Harry! In just a moment we'll wheel them in.

53. The doctor told Harry to give up wine, women, and song. Harry said, "I don't sing anyway." The doctor said, "Good, now give up one more: will it be wine or women?" Harry said, "That will depend on the particular vintage."

54. Harry thinks he's a "Hot Pistol"; says he feels like a young colt; maybe, but he still looks like an old 45.

55. Harry likes being sixty. A young woman referred to him as a sexagenarian and he figures at this stage of his life, that's the closest he'll get to flattery.

56. Harry's better now, but a few years ago we almost lost him: nearly overdosed on Geritol.

57. Harry, you look like a million. Of course, we all know you couldn't be that old.

58. He's at that stage of life when the mind says, "Go! Go! Go!" and the body says, "No! No! No!"

59. The Missile Age has taken its toll on Harry. All this talk of nuclear balance just upsets him. He told me once, "I

felt safer in the mid-thirties when all I had to fear was fear itself."

5. Family

1. His son is the image of him; oh well, as long as the kid is healthy.

2. His wife told me that on their honeymoon she stole all the towels out of their hotel room, just so it wouldn't be a total loss.

3. Harry proved that breaking up is hard to do, but that getting together in the first place is even tougher.

4. Harry's wife thought she married for mink, but all she got was a little weasel.

5. Harry never put his foot down, because he doesn't want it stepped on.

6. Harry's wife said he came home a little the worse for wear last night; came up the driveway much too fast, banged into the garage doors and knocked one of them off its hinges. She said, "Thank God he didn't have the car."

7. Because of his many business interests, Harry incorporated himself with his wife and parents as business partners. He was upset recently when they got together and forced him out of the firm.

8. Harry was surprised when his wife gave him a bottle of musk oil for his birthday. He says he didn't even know his musk squeaked.

9. I had to deliver a package to Harry's house one morning around 5:00 A.M. so he could take it on an early flight. There was no one up so I pounded on the door until someone opened an upstairs window and yelled "What do you want?" "Is this Harry Gordon's house?" I asked. "Yes," they yelled back, "Just leave him on the porch."

10. Harry's such a romantic: his wife tells us that he once

said: "My love for you surpasses anything else that's offered in that particular line."

11. Harry's always the complete negotiator. I remember the time one of his kids asked for an ice cream and Harry said: "Don't ask for anything until you're twenty-one and I'll buy you a car."

12. His daughter told me about the time her fiancé asked Harry for permission to marry her. Harry said: "So, you want to be my son-in-law, eh?" and the boy said "Not really, but if I marry your daughter, there's no way around it."

13. His wife told me that they've been married for seventeen years and she hasn't spoken a single word to him in that time. I said, "My God, what's wrong?" and she said, "Nothing, I just didn't want to interrupt him."

14. Harry's family fortune was lost in the crash of 1929 when a New York stockbroker leaped from the tenth floor of his Wall Street office and landed smack on Harry's father's pushcart.

15. His wife finally cured him of nail biting. She hides his teeth.

16. Harry's wife says she married a banker and a warm, sensitive human being. Sounds like bigamy to me.

17. Or as his wife says to him: "Harry, for once you're wrong . . . again."

18. His father-in-law didn't want his girl to marry a writer; but after he read some of Harry's stuff, he dropped his objections.

19. Harry thinks his wife may be getting tired of him: she's started wrapping his lunch in road maps.

20. His wife says she has to handle all the decorating chores herself. Seems the only thing Harry ever bought for the house was a round of drinks.

21. Harry's the only guy I know who paid $1,000 to research his family tree, and then paid $2,000 to hush it up.

22. When you talk about heavy drinkers, though, his Uncle Tim has to take the prize. Poor Tim, rest his soul, drank a fifth of Irish with each of his three meals, then took a nightcap at bedtime. When he finally died, the family tried to honor his last wish by having him cremated. It took them three days to get the fire out.

23. And his Uncle Pat was another case; he worked for Guinness and died, poor man, after he slipped and fell into a vat of stout he was working near. Three times they sent rescue crews in to get him, and three times he fought them off.

24. In speaking of Uncle Pat, the family used to say he wasn't exactly a policeman, but he did go with them a lot.

25. Poor Harry; he was so embarrassed at the registration desk today. He came in late and saw a woman who, from the back, looked like his wife. He walked up, put his arms around her, and kissed her on the neck. When he realized what he had done, he said, "I'm terribly sorry, you look just like my wife." She said, "Get away from me, creep!" and he said, "Gee, you talk just like her too."

26. His wife said their doctor told them both to get more exercise. So Harry took up golfing, and he lets her caddy.

27. He won't marry until he finds some girl who likes what he likes: him.

28. Harry's not into the social scene. His wife says a big night out is when they sit on the porch and watch TV through the window.

29. Did you ever read Harry's family tree? He has roots back:

To old Noah Gordon who said, "Thank God it floats!"

To Helen of Troy Gordon who said, "That's all Paris has to offer?"

To Adam Gordon who told his wife, "I didn't cheat on you. Count my ribs!"

And to Christopher Columbus Gordon who said, "I don't know where I'm going, but I'm making good time!"

30. Harry told his wife that he needed to get away for a few days . . . alone. She was very understanding. She booked him on a cruise . . . into the Bermuda Triangle.

31. Harry's son-in-law tells about the time he asked Harry for permission to marry his daughter. The boy was nervous, and he said, "Mr. Gordon, I've been dating your daughter for three years now," and Harry said, "So? You want a pension?"

32. Harry never married because he was saving himself for "Miss Right." Isn't that sweet? I never knew Orville and Wilbur had a sister.

33. Harry's wife bought a dress for the dinner tonight. Like it? The clerk told her it was $500 dollars and she guaranteed a fit. And she was right: Harry is having the fit right now.

34. I was at his wedding, and when he said the part about ". . . with all my worldly goods I thee endow. . ." someone in back shouted, "Well Harry, there goes the bicycle!"

35. Did he ever tell you how his Uncle Tim lost two fingers? He worked in a sawmill. One day he yelled to the foreman, "I just lost a finger!" The foreman said, "How?" Tim said, "I was reaching across like this and . . . damn! There goes another one!"

36. Harry has a family of all girls. He was hoping for a boy to help him with the housework.

37. The school took Harry's little boy to the zoo with his class and they stopped in front of the deer pen. Harry's little boy said, "What's that?" The teacher said, "Guess, what does mommy call daddy?" and the little kid said, "Wow, that's a louse?"

38. When they swore him in for jury duty, the judge asked him if he had formed or expressed any recent opinions.

Harry looked at his wife and said, "No judge, not for the past seventeen years."

39. His wife thinks Harry married her because he needed someone to blame outside the office as well.

40. Harry has a family tradition. Every time he goes on a trip, he brings his wife a little present. He even does it when he has no reason to feel guilty.

41. I asked Harry's wife if she saw any difference in his drinking since he went to the shrink. She said, "Yes, now he only drinks on the couch."

42. We'll be brief, Harry. We know that tonight is the night you get your semi-annual "urge" . . . and also the night that Mrs. Harry gets her semi-annual headache.

43. Some of Harry's problems started back in the old days. There wasn't a lot of money and the kids had to swap clothes and wear hand-me-downs. It was tougher for Harry than it was for his four sisters.

44. It's no wonder Harry has a complex. His father spent the first few years of Harry's life looking for a loophole in the birth certificate.

45. Harry stayed single all these years. He says that although a man doesn't understand true happiness until he's married, by then it's too late.

46. Harry and his wife just had a discussion over whether they should buy him a new car, or her a fur coat. They compromised: they bought her the fur coat, but she lets him keep it in the garage.

47. Harry says that he lays the law down to his wife. Naturally, he agrees to accept all her amendments.

48. His Uncle Al was a stockbroker. He went for a physical once and the doctor said his blood pressure was 170. Al said, "When it hits 200, sell!" Al didn't have to worry though. When it hit 180, he got it to split two for one.

49. His Uncle Shaun was a bookie in Boston. He wrote all

his bets in Latin. The Irish cops couldn't bother him: every bet looked like a prayer.

50. He said that for Christmas his wife wanted a little car of her own, but he bought her furs and jewels instead. I said, "Why jewels and furs if she wanted a car?" He said, "Who sells imitation cars?"

51. Harry says that when he was a boy, his mother loved him. He could tell because she only hit him with the soft end of the mop.

6. Education

1. He took a speed reading course and read the entire Bible cover to cover in fourteen minutes; said it was something about God.

2. Not everyone who comes from (place) automatically goes to (school). If you know the right people, you can get out of it.

3. He asked me to pick up a book at the library; he said it was something about a "red boat or a scarlet ship"; it was the *Rubaiyat.*

4. He said he'd have been an M.D. by now if it wasn't for one thing: the AMA.

5. So we sent him to language school. Here's his bill from Berlitz: $500 for French, $500 for Spanish, and $1000 for Scotch.

6. He had to have a B.A., an M.A., an M.B.A., and a Ph.D. before he got a J.O.B.

7. Harry's wife tells me that he helps the little kids with their homework almost every night. I guess he's trying to get past the "Help Stage" before the kids hit high school.

8. Harry is an example to us all: he does not smoke, nor drink, nor run around; nor is there any evidence at all of his ever taking a mind-expanding drug.

9. People who complain that we spend more money on (li-

quor, athletics, clothes, etc.) than we do on education don't realize how much we can learn from a guy like Harry.

10. I can honestly say that in all the years I've known him, no one has ever questioned Harry's intelligence. In fact, I've never heard anyone mention it.

11. Harry has several degrees. Our only worry is that he might have been educated beyond his intelligence.

12. When Harry was a young boy in school, he was teacher's pet. She couldn't afford a dog.

13. Harry has a typical engineering background: graduated from R.P.I. at the age of seven and earned his master's and doctorate at M.I.T. two years later. Worked for Dr. Goddard for a while, but they split after a nasty disagreement over a telemetry formula. Harry didn't carry a grudge. He said Dr. Goddard later found his mistake and apologized.

14. When Harry graduated, the class voted him most likely to go to seed.

15. You may wonder what is the difference between Harry's college and an asylum. Well, you must noticeably improve before you can get out of the asylum.

16. Always looking for the easy way out. He used to play hooky from correspondence school: sent in empty envelopes.

17. His drinking even got him into trouble during medical school. It was bad enough that he drank the formaldehyde; but he wasn't spitting out the specimens.

18. Harry tries to compensate for a lack of formal education by making up little stories to impress his friends. He told me once that he had read Shakespeare in the original French.

19. A college education from (name) seldom hurts a man . . . as long as he's willing to learn a little something afterwards.

20. They say that God doesn't check for degrees, titles, net worth or decorations. He checks for scars.

21. Harry told his boss that he had taken his business plan right out of a B School textbook. His boss said, "You were right to do that, Harry, it obviously didn't belong there."

22. You know how Harry talks about his years at Harvard? He worked a few years for the medical school as a resurrectionist.

23. Harry thought highly of education until just recently when he flunked that course in sensitivity training. He is in a remedial group now.

24. When he got out of college, he took an aptitude test. The examiner told him: "You have a splendid future in any field where a close relative holds a senior management position."

25. Harry stayed in his home town until he was twenty-six. He wanted to finish high school.

26. Harry is such a culture snob since he took that wine appreciation course. When he went in for that surgery last month, he made the surgeon promise to only open him at room temperature.

27. Harry attended (name) University where he was a four-letter man. (Pause) I'll bet three of those letters were "S.O.B."

28. What an education! Sometimes I think that if learning were money, Harry would need a short-term loan to buy coffee.

29. At the school he graduated from, they won't give you a letter until you prove you can read one.

7. Position

1. What a man of business. Crime wouldn't pay if we let him run it.

2. When I came here, I knew nothing about (product) but

(boss) said, "Don't worry, you'll have people on your staff who know all about it." He was wrong.

3. He does the work of two men: Laurel and Hardy.

4. Some businessman: He thought margins were the heavy black lines you had to stay between when you color.

5. (Name) is his immediate superior; but then, anybody would be his immediate superior.

6. When I first went to work for Harry, I was a poor struggling (job title). He helped me get used to it.

7. Talk about single-minded dedication to business: he walked into my office one day last week and told me one of our salesmen just died. "My God," I said, "What did he have?" "Not much," he answered, "just a couple of OEMs and a small End User."

8. Organizational genius? He once fouled up a two-car funeral.

9. He said to (boss), "I'll bet a hundred dollars you won't pick me for that job"; (Boss) took the bet and raised him a hundred.

10. They say he's not too bright. I ask you: Would we have our jobs if he were any smarter?

11. We made him a VP so he could carry out our corporate plan. We never thought he'd carry them out on a stretcher.

12. The company installed the new boiler under the (name) department so if it blew up before 10:00 A.M. or after 4:00 P.M., no one would get hurt.

13. The boss said, "I've got to find someone for this big job." Harry said "How about me?" The boss said, "No thanks, I'll have to do the looking myself."

14. Salesman's mentality? I once saw him add 15 and 15 and get 100. I asked him about the extra 70 and he said "follow on potential."

15. He feels about (boss) like statues feel about pigeons.

16. I am proud to work for Harry . . . but I could be just as proud on half the grief.

17. When Harry got promoted to Vice President, a friend told him not to take it too seriously: A & P Supermarkets have a Vice President in charge of vegetables. Well, Harry didn't believe that so when he was alone he called A & P and said, "Let me speak to the VP in charge of vegetables." The operator said, "Yes, sir, would that be fresh, canned, or frozen vegetables?"

18. I was going to visit the headquarters building complex and I asked Harry which side the Law Department was on. He said, "Ours, I think."

19. I'd like to think of Harry as a teacher, a man who instructs by example. Watching Harry, for example, you learn the difference between twenty-five years of experience and one year . . . twenty-five times.

20. Harry, when they read the roster of all time great managers, you'll be right there, listening.

21. At least you can be thankful Harry, that you'll never be replaced by automation. No self-respecting computer would ever want a job like that.

22. If you work around Harry, you learn to do bird imitations. For example, I watch him like a hawk.

23. Harry wasn't born to power and greatness. He had power and greatness thrust upon him. Too bad he ducked.

24. Offering people legal advice gives Harry a grand and glorious feeling. You give him the grand and that gives him a glorious feeling.

25. Harry is one of the most highly suspected people in the entire company.

26. He wants everything to be checked with him first. Last

November I heard his secretary say: "Next Thursday is Thanksgiving, Harry, if that's okay with you."

27. It took a lot of years, but the Personnel Department finally got Harry to take an aptitude test. It turned out he was best suited for retirement. The rest of us knew that years ago.

28. What's it like working for a guy like Harry? Some guys named their first ulcer after him.

29. Two of our founders fought a duel over Harry some years ago and they both got him. One got him in the arm and the other got him in the leg.

30. Harry is always willing to let a manager run his own show . . . as long as Harry writes the script and directs.

31. Nobody knows exactly who Harry reports to. He says he's got an unlisted boss.

32. He runs the MIS Department . . . sometimes called the House of Ill Compute.

33. Harry's back was against the wall for so long that the handwriting was on him.

34. Harry was really upset last week. He answered his phone and some woman said "Is this the gas company?" Harry said, "No, it is not, this is the (name) Department." The woman thought for a second and said, "Well, I didn't miss it by much, did I?"

35. I told him once, "Harry, Rome wasn't built in a day." He said, "I didn't run that job."

36. The people who work for Harry wish he were Pope. Then they'd only have to kiss his ring. I don't know though; Harry would keep that ring in his back pocket.

37. When people apply for work at our firm, they are given an intelligence test. The top five percent get assigned to the Forward Planning Group. The bottom five percent get assigned to (name of Harry's department).

38. I enjoy working for Harry ... being his assistant ... sitting in for him at meetings ... in fact, the only thing that ever bothered me was going to the dentist for him.

39. Harry is proud of his unofficial role as Corporate Advisor. He told me once that when he gives a person advice, it's all they need to last a lifetime. I asked "How do you know that?" He answered, "Well, they never come back."

40. Harry takes credit for a lot of accomplishments ... mine mostly.

41. Harry knows a great deal about the field of (subject). He just forgot most of it.

42. Harry is in charge of our corporate travel policy. Do you all understand how that works? Take travel on Air-India for example. They have three classes. In Brahmin Class you have a sit-down gourmet dinner served on silver. In Business Class you get a superb Indian buffet on fine china. Harry has us traveling as Untouchables. They just give you a wooden bowl and you beg from the first two classes.

43. Harry came to the firm very highly recommended by his previous employers. He had letters of recommendation from Larry, Moe, and Curly.

44. Harry knows how to get along with the boss. I was in his office last week when the boss called and Harry said "yes sir" sixteen times straight. Then he said "no sir" once and hung up. I said "Harry, what was that last question?" Harry said, "Oh, he just asked if I disagreed with anything he had said."

45. I'm not going to say anything offensive about Harry. Like most people who work for him, my relationship goes beyond Love and Respect. My relationship is based on Fear.

46. There are a lot of people who believe in Harry . . . there are a lot of people who believe in the Easter Bunny.

47. Harry made big money years ago as a publicity agent. Corporations, entertainers, charities, all paid Harry thousands to get their names in front of the public. He personally handled United Silicon Emissions, Inc., the talented and lovely Rosemary Pandrolis, and the entire Foundation for the Cure of Styleman's Disease.

48. I asked one of his people if they listen to Harry. "A little," the guy said, "but not enough to affect my performance."

49. Harry just called me aside to correct something I said earlier; as a Publicity Agent he did have one famous client: The Unknown Soldier.

50. People who work for Harry during Lent have a real problem; what else is there to give up?

51. They installed the new air conditioning unit on the roof over Harry's department. That way if the roof collapses before 10:00 A.M. or after 4:00 P.M., no one will be hurt.

52. He spent his entire business career clawing his way to . . . the middle.

53. They say he knows his job so well he can do it backwards . . . perhaps that's the problem!

54. When things go wrong on the job and you see Harry smile, you know he's just found someone to blame.

55. Harry, on the job, is sort of like the piano player in a bordello. He's near the action but he doesn't get totally involved.

56. (If Harry works for a woman) I was an early victim of sexual harassment.

57. (If Harry is an Administrative Executive) Harry is in charge of P & L: Parking Lots and Latrines.

58. Folks back home always said that the best lawyer in

town was Harry Gordon, when he was sober. They said the second best lawyer was Harry Gordon when he was drunk.

59. The way Harry runs his security, I'm never sure if he's trying to keep new ideas in ... or out.

60. Harry left his previous employer because of illness; he got sick of him.

61. Harry is about 44 around the chest, 38 around the hips, 100 around the golf course, and a pain around the office.

62. How can the bosses expect Harry to lose any weight when they're always making him eat his words?

63. Harry told the boss: "I spend almost all my waking hours on this job." The boss said: "I believe that Harry, but you still have to put in a minimum of eight each day."

64. Because I helped arrange this Roast, Harry called me a "Judas." That's not true, Harry. Judas got thirty pieces of silver. I sold you out for the fun of it.

65. Does he pay well? They call it "take home pay" because that's about the only place you can go with it.

66. Harry's been around a long time. His first job was as Project Manager on Noah's Ark. He didn't like it; said they were a bunch of animals.

67. When Harry interviewed me for this job, he asked if I could keep my mouth shut and follow orders to the letter. I said, "Yes sir!" Harry said, "Good, and don't ever interrupt me like that again!"

68. Harry's staff meetings are fascinating to attend: He talks, nobody listens, then they all disagree.

69. If there really is such a thing as "supply and demand," how do you explain all the consultants?

70. Consultants in the company are a bit like eunuchs in the harem; they're present when it's done, get to see

it done, even talk to the folks who are doing it, but somehow they never get to do it themselves.

71. Harry's salary reviews are always a classic. Once he said to the boss: "You could promote a man like me." The boss thought about that for a minute and said: "Yes, if he wasn't too much like you."

72. You all know that Harry is continually late for work. Well, one day the boss had to warn him about it. Harry was so upset, he went right home, had dinner, went to bed, got up at 6:00 A.M. and was at his desk by 8:00 A.M. When the boss walked by, Harry said, "I guess I'm on time today!" The boss said, "Yes, but where were you yesterday?"

73. I tried to see Harry one day last week and his secretary said: "He can't see anyone, he has a sore back." I said: "Tell him I want to talk, not wrestle."

74. (Name) is Harry's assistant. His job is to keep Harry on the straight and narrow. His last job was with the circus yanking raw meat away from the lions.

75. Harry worked for Western Union as a young man and had a brilliant career ahead of him until his voice changed.

76. Actually, Western Union could have solved that problem for Harry but he declined the operation on religious grounds.

77. Harry says that missing your goals is just a misdemeanor; the more you miss, da meaner he gets.

78. Harry was in charge of compensation plans for a while, a position he tormented for several years. He told me once the mark of a good comp plan is simplicity. I forget the plan he had me on. Something about multiplying my social security number by my zip code and getting paid in Hong Kong dollars every Shrove Tuesday.

79. They're a dull group back there in Engineering. Harry

chartered an airplane for a departmental trip once. They gave him a boring 727.

80. When Harry originally applied for work here, management called him "A First Round Draft Choice." That means they hoped the Army would get him first.

81. How can you argue high technology with a guy who still doesn't put his full weight down when he flies?

82. Is Harry difficult to work for? He's got the only personal computer that has to go back to the shop for counseling.

83. Harry's department would remind you of a snowstorm: No two flakes are alike.

84. Harry calls them as he sees them. The boss asked him for an honest forecast and Harry told him: "I can be honest or I can give you a forecast, but not both."

85. His employees just named him in a class action intimidation suit.

86. It's the age of overspecialization. I met a doctor the other day who specializes in diseases of the nose; left nostril.

87. The little birds told about the lawyer (cheap, cheap), but the little ducks talk about the doctor.

88. His wife told me she knows he's good to his employees. Every night in his sleep he says things like "I'll raise you fifty."

89. When I was married, I took an oath to love, honor, and obey. I took that oath again when I came to work for Harry.

90. They work together like a football team with no quarterback and four footballs.

91. Who else but a lawyer could write a twenty-five page document and then call it a brief?

92. He said my employment contract would be a Gentleman's Agreement. In other words, he didn't want to put anything in writing.

93. When he called to offer me the job, I was almost too excited to accept the charges.

94. He got a pretty good idea of the position's level within the firm when they asked him if he could type.

95. He said he's pursuing his career. I guess "pursue" is the right word. He's certainly way behind.

96. His talks are alternately like the Peace of God and the Love of God. The Peace of God in that they surpass all understanding, and the Love of God in that they endure forever.

97. He worked twelve years for the Hanes Underwear Company where he was known as Inspector 6.

98. I asked him if my group got into trouble how much time did I have to make it right. He said, "The rest of your career."

99. As a public speaker he was a cyclone . . . that's a vacuum surrounded by high winds.

100. A job like (some bureaucratic position) is probably the nearest thing to immortality that a company offers.

101. Some of us are appointed to our positions. Some of us are anointed. . .

102. He said he was a diamond cutter. That means he mowed the lawn on a ball field.

103. He's such a clever attorney. He once got a client on annulment on the basis that her father wasn't licensed to carry the shotgun.

104. Talking to (name) about (name's subject) is like trying to give a fish a bath.

105. Harry's got a computer down there in (department) that is so intelligent and sophisticated that it will blame its mistakes on the computer it replaced.

106. Harry could work for any boss he pleased. Unfortunately, he didn't please any one of them.

107. You can't help liking Harry. If you don't he fires you.

108. Harry didn't quite make it as an auditor. He used to

look at a company's balance sheet and if the total assets and total liabilities were exactly the same, he figured everything must be all right.

109. When I first started working for him, Harry didn't spend a lot of time with me. I remember thinking that if I was found dead in my office he wouldn't be able to identify the body.

110. Years ago Harry worked for the (name) company, but he left them abruptly. He said he wouldn't work for a boss who said "get out and stay out."

111. I asked Harry to do some personal work for me once and I gave him a $100 advance. He said that entitled me to two questions. I said: "Two questions for $100? Isn't that rather high?" Harry said: "Yes, it is; what's your second question?"

112. I asked his secretary (name) how she could be so organized and happy working all those years for Harry. She said: "Simple; I don't listen."

113. Harry was never much of a salesman. In fact, he couldn't talk a customer out of a burning building.

114. What a salesman! He could talk a hungry dog off a meat wagon.

115. If you've ever worried about reincarnation, walk through Harry's department some day around 5:00 P.M. and watch them all coming back to life.

116. Harry once told me the ideal contract is made up of words too big to understand, and print too small to read.

117. Morale in Harry's department is a continuing problem. Personnel did a survey over there last month: sixty percent said they liked Harry, thirty-five percent said they didn't like him, the other five percent beat up the guy taking the survey.

118. What was it like working for Harry? It was like string-

ing pearls . . . with no knot in the other end of the thread.

119. In his younger years Harry wanted to be a doctor, but had to give it up when he learned he couldn't stand the sight of money.

120. When I took over from Harry, he told me that some days would be tough, and he gave me three sealed and numbered envelopes which he said would carry me through when I was in really deep trouble and could use some good advice.

    I was in trouble a few weeks later, and I opened Envelope #1. It read: "Blame the previous manager." I took that advice and things went okay for a while, but then the trouble started again, worse than before, and I had to open Envelope #2. It read: "Blame the (name) department." I took that advice and things went okay for a very little while and then the trouble really started up again, this time worse than ever. I had to open Envelope #3. It read simply: "Prepare three envelopes."

121. Harry sold the very first (latest product). The only problem is that he sold it five years ago.

122. After retirement from here, Harry is going to strike out on a whole new career experience and try something he's never done before: He's going to take a regular job and work eight hours each day.

123. Before he came to us, Harry worked in several different fields. He worked in a wheat field, a potato field, and a cotton field.

124. Harry's secretary told me that a lot of his visitors must be from California. I asked why and she said, "Well, as they leave they always mumble something about the sun and the beach."

125. Harry likes to run around a lot. I heard him tell the boss: "I made fifteen sales calls yesterday! I could have

made even more but some jerk wanted to know what I was selling."

126. Harry's on another diet. It seems he walked into a clothing store and said to the clerk: "I'd like to see a bathing suit in my size," and the clerk said, "So would I."

127. Well, at least we're all protected against loss by fire and damage. Every single piece of equipment is covered by insurance. Except for the clock, and Harry watches that.

128. I was with Harry one day last week when Accounting called him about his expense reports. They understood air travel, meals, car rental, etc., but every so often there's an entry like "$50 G.O.K." or "$100 G.O.K.", and they wanted to know what G.O.K. meant. Harry told them that he sometimes loses receipts and it means "God Only Knows."

129. Harry is such a shrewd motivator: I recently asked him for a raise and he turned me down . . . but agreed to name his computer terminal after me.

130. I remember the time I met Harry as he was leaving his boss's staff meeting and he said: "I feel like telling that guy off again!" I said, "Again?" and Harry said "Yes, I felt like telling him off last week, too."

131. Is Harry insecure? No, but the people who work for him are.

132. He left his last position for what the papers called "Irreconcilable Management Differences." That means he wanted to stay, but they said he couldn't.

133. It's not my fault I'm growing bald: Harry needed a hair transplant and he selected me to be the donor.

134. Harry looks so happy when he comes to work at 8:30 each morning. I asked his secretary about it and she said: "Well, it's about the only time the poor man can tell himself that he hasn't made a single mistake all day."

135. Harry used to say, "I take orders from no one." That's what cost him a career in the Sales Department.

136. Our office is like a finely tuned assembly line: (name) designs the unit, (name) puts the parts on the moving belt, (name) puts on the sides and top, (name) puts on the bottom with the nuts and bolts which hold it all together, and Harry lies on his back . . . and screws up all day.

137. Working for Harry makes you wonder sometimes if you can ever win. Well, the answer is: you can win . . . it's just not likely.

138. When I first met Harry I was unemployed and at peace with the world. He changed both of those things.

139. The sign on his office door reads "10 to 4." Those aren't his hours; those are the odds against finding him in.

140. Harry is an investment banker. That's the kind of guy who'd want to marry Bo Derek so he could get his hands on her money.

141. Harry doesn't personally have ulcers, but he is a carrier.

142. Harry wanted a job in long-range planning. He figured that by the time he was proved wrong, he'd already be on pension.

143. Harry is a financial consultant. A consultant . . . that's a guy who knows 100 ways to make love but has never gone out with a girl.

144. Harry is a hard-nosed businessman and although he has a reputation for honesty, piety, and love of his fellow man, these character defects do not detract from his ability to terrorize employees, intimidate vendors, and stampede customers into a buying decision.

145. Harry has an even disposition: He's miserable all the time.

146. They say that God doesn't count against your life the hours you've spent fishing. On the other hand, God

gives you an eighteen-month bonus for every year you've spent working with Harry.

147. Harry just spoke about the challenges facing us over the next year. I just wish we knew as little about them as he does.

148. When I started working for Harry, he used to change his managers around pretty quickly. We didn't mind having our name written on the door with chalk, but the damp sponge hanging from the doorknob was too much.

149. At the start of his staff meeting Harry tells us: "Say all your ideas and suggestions now, before my valium wears off."

150. Someone said, "Harry gets so much mail, how does he keep up with it?" Well, we know the secret. He stamps it "Please Handle" and sends it to us.

151. Harry delegates so well, he once got me to sit in for him at his annual physical.

152. Harry just introduced a new flexible-hours program. You can come in any time you want before eight, and leave whenever you please after five.

153. Harry's boss just threatened a major reorganization: He found out we have more vice presidents than customers.

154. When Harry made out his will, he asked me to be a pall-bearer. Well, I guess I can carry him a little further.

155. He used to work for the competition. You know their slogan: "The Quality Goes in Before the Name Falls Off."

156. There were times in his early years when Harry wished he had gone to work for his father; but he had always been allergic to the monkey.

157. Harry will never work for another family owned business. He still remembers the day the boss brought his

six-year-old son in and Harry found himself thinking: "What a nice little kid . . . I'm going to enjoy working for him."

158. Harry may be too outspoken for a family company; like the day he called the boss's son a "walking advertisement for a 100 percent inheritance tax."

159. People wonder why the boss gave Harry a corner office with a window. Now the story can be told. Part of Harry's job is to watch the highway and immediately warn everyone to evacuate the building if he sees the glaciers coming back.

160. I asked him one day, "Harry, do you know anything about banking?" and he said, "Oh, one or two funny stories."

161. I won't cross Harry because I believe in him. Also, winter is coming on and I'm too old for outside work.

162. Harry's staff meeting would remind you of a carousel ride: lots of activity, movement, and sound but not much forward progress. Nobody gets the gold ring either.

163. One time Harry said that he had just told the boss where to get off; he pointed out all his mistakes and wondered aloud if he was really capable of running the operation. I said, "Wow, what did he say?" and Harry said, "Nothing. I hung up before he recognized my voice."

164. After one of his cases, he went home while the jury was out and his partner called, yelling: "Justice has triumphed!" and Harry said, "Shut up and start the appeal!"

165. Harry uses statistics like a drunk uses a lamppost: more for support than illumination.

166. One of the guys from another division showed up for Harry's afternoon staff meeting with a few too many under his belt. He said to the receptionist: "Is thish

the way to get to Harry's staff meeting?" She looked at him for a minute and said: "Pal, that's the only way to go to Harry's staff meeting."

167. I asked Harry if I was kidnapped, would the company ransom me. He said not if it meant breaking a twenty.

168. Harry's managers abroad publish a picture of themselves under a picture of Harry in the local press. The copy says: "If you kidnap the men in the bottom picture, you must deal with the man in the top picture."

169. Harry's group reminds me of a snow storm; no two flakes are quite alike.

170. At his last staff meeting the boss said: "We're a perfect blend of talents, just like an athlete's body: Management is the brain, Sales is the eyes, Manufacturing is the hands, Marketing the legs that keep us ahead of the competition ..." Harry jumped up and said, "What part of the body am I?" You shouldn't tempt a person like that, Harry.

171. At the last corporate reception a guy came up to Harry three times with all sorts of complaints about Harry's operation. Finally, Harry said to (name): "That guy is really bothering me." (Name said: "Ignore him, Harry, he just repeats what everyone else is saying."

172. Harry was a consultant. That's a guy who quit work but kept the breaks and lunch.

173. The company was so concerned about Harry's happiness that they hired a detective to learn the reason for it.

174. A (Harry's profession) intellectual is one who can listen to the *William Tell* Overture without thinking of the Lone Ranger.

175. It's not easy writing speeches for Harry: you are limited to words and concepts that he understands.

176. Harry has much to say on both sides of an issue and, much to our regret, he always does.

177. Whenever you listen to all the terrible things they say about each other, the safest course is always to believe that both sides are speaking the truth.

178. Once he told (name), "Stop yawning when I talk to you!" (Name) said, "I wasn't yawning, I was trying to say something!"

179. He says he's a doctor of Laws. Well, if anybody ever doctored the law, I guess it's him.

180. He can say things so beautifully. Once at a restaurant, he became physically ill and couldn't get out in time. He said, "I'm afraid I'm going to have to bring up something unpleasant."

181. Harry says that the biggest difference between TV news and a newspaper is that tomorrow you can wrap your garbage in the newspaper.

182. Some guys are tried and found wanting; Harry wanted and was found trying.

183. Harry always begins his sales lectures by saying, "Is there anyone here who thinks he'll fail? If so, stand up now!" Last week, after a pause, a young guy stood up. Harry says, "Are you a damn fool who wants to fail?" The young guy says, "No sir, I just hated to see you stand there alone."

184. He told me about the early days when he was a computer trouble-shooter. He'd visit the client, walk up to the computer, open the door, and go inside. Then he'd replace the bad tube.

185. Harry said he learned an important lesson in all those years of teaching: If you get a wise kid who argues with you, tries to trip you up logically, dissects and disagrees, don't put him down too harshly. He may be the only one who's listening.

186. If we ever want a company zoo, we'll just fence you in.

187. His mother told us about the day Harry overslept for school. "Get up, Harry," she said. "I don't want to,"

said Harry. "What you want doesn't matter," said his mother, "get up and go to school!" "Why should I?" asked Harry. "Because," says his mother, "you're forty-eight years old and you're the principal!"

188. Harry, your entire group was tested by the personnel department, and I just got your test results tonight! Your group has an average IQ of . . . 200! Wait! Darn this light! That word isn't "average," it's "cumulative."

189. Personnel called and told him they needed a list of our sales people, broken down by sex. Harry told them, "Booze is more of a problem here."

190. Remember when he ran for office and they had that big debate? His opponent yelled, "What about the powerful interests who control you?" and Harry shot right back, "Let's leave wives out of this!"

191. Sometimes Harry, I think that if we took all our economists, forecasters, business planners, and laid them all end to end, they'd still point in all directions.

192. The only thing any magazine ever accepted from him was a subscription form.

193. I came in one day and found Harry arguing price with a vendor. I said, "Harry, why bother? You won't pay him anyway." Harry said, "True, but he's a nice guy and I want him to keep his losses down."

194. He goes to the airport, lays down his air travel card, and says, "Give me a ticket to anyplace . . . it doesn't matter . . . I have business all over."

195. He pays so little attention to me that if I died, he wouldn't be able to identify the body.

196. Harry is a model boss. Unfortunately, he is not a working model.

197. I asked him how much the operation would cost and he said $500. I asked, "Is it dangerous?" He said, "Non-

sense! You can't buy a dangerous operation for a mere $500."

198. Last winter his car was stuck in a snowbank, he told me, and he got it out by tying a cat to the bumper and motivating the cat to pull the car out of the snow bank. I said, "Harry, how can you motivate a cat to do that?" He says, "Same way I motivate you, I have a whip."

199. He tries to be all things to all people. For example, four of us met today to decide an issue. (Name) said we should do it. Harry said, "You are right!" Then, (name #2) said we should not do it, and Harry said, "You are right too!" I said, "Harry, they can't both be right." And Harry said, "How right you are!"

200. Last weekend he had to hire a plumber, and when it came time to settle up, the guy wanted one hundred bucks an hour! Harry said, "One hundred bucks an hour? Why, I'm a lawyer and I only charge fifty!" and the plumber said, "Yeah, that's all I charged when I was a lawyer."

201. To hear Harry talk, he's been about everything and done about everything. We ought to send him out for a group photo.

202. Once we were traveling across Canada; it was Harry's first trip there, and we stopped in this little cocktail lounge for a drink. There was a very attractive young woman sitting there alone so Harry walked over and said, "Hello, I'm new to Canada, where are you from?" The young woman smiled and answered, "Saskatoon, Saskatchewan." Harry looked at me and said, "My God, she can't even speak English!"

203. Harry says one of the great truths of sales is "never tell someone more than you think they'll believe."

204. Harry's career may be compared to a game of golf. He

no sooner gets out of one hole than he goes looking for another.

205. Last night during a council meeting, he fell asleep and only woke up when an environmental group started chanting, "We Want Clean Water!" Harry said, "Okay! Okay! But just a little in mine."

206. Harry was in the theatre for many years. I'll never forget hearing him mouth those famous words: "Popcorn! Peanuts! Cracker Jacks!"

207. I'm Harry's assistant. If anything happens to him, I'm the guy you'll have to bury.

208. Harry brings a religious zeal to the business of sales. I asked him once if this was his territory. He said, "No, it's my diocese."

209. Harry would have made a fortune in this business, if it weren't for all the damn competition.

210. He's just so damn imaginative! When Harry's creative juices get flowing, just clear the decks for action! Here's one of his recent ventures. He met a man named Irving Cola and tried to convince him to go into a partnership with Imogene Coca, and market a new soft drink based on the combination of their names: "Imogene Irving"!

211. Harry has changed jobs so many times that his skin is beginning to fade from all those employee badge photographs.

212. First an announcement for you folks in Harry's department. A little later there will be a couple of jokes about kissing Harry's ring. They are just jokes! I say that because I don't want anyone to be trampled in the rush.

213. Harry used to think up compensation plans for us in sales. He said the essence of a good plan was simplicity. I remember the one he had me on. You multiplied your age by your ZIP code, subtracted your area code, and got paid half that in Hong Kong dollars every Ash Wednesday.

214. Harry is my family attorney. He advises my family, and I support his.

215. Harry will not run for public office. He couldn't stand any job where the public knew what his salary was.

216. Harry won't even let his kids play cops and robbers. He makes them play cops and alleged perpetrators.

217. He sent one article to the *Atlantic* and they kept it. They didn't publish it; they just didn't want it in circulation.

218. It was Harry who taught us the legal maxim that has guided us these many years: Every man is innocent until proven bankrupt.

219. We've enjoyed every one of your little homilies, Reverend Harry. Why, we never really knew what sin was until you came here!

220. And Harry has given us employee benefits! Yes, benefits! Like life insurance! Have you read your policy, friends? The benefit is that if we die, our families no longer have to pay the premiums!

221. I work for Harry and people constantly ask me, what's the secret of teaching an old dog new tricks? The answer is obvious. You just have to know more than the old dog.

222. Harry feels sure that he has lived before. In a prior life he was Damage Control Officer on the Titanic.

8. Personal Characteristics

1. They say he's outspoken . . . but by whom?

2. He says he's tough . . . when he was in fifth grade he could beat up all the kids his own age. He never had a fight. The kids his own age were in high school.

3. Some guys can talk for hours on a subject. He doesn't need a subject.

4. He's changing his religion: He no longer believes he's God.

5. I remember the time one of his guys died at his desk. Actually, the poor guy just collapsed, but by the time Harry got bids from three ambulance services, he was gone.

6. He was so lazy that when you looked "lazy" up in the dictionary you found his picture.

7. In a company of workaholics, he's been on the wagon for years.

8. He's a Sweet Old Boy. We call him by his initials.

9. He has a lot. He just can't remember where he put it.

10. Someone asked if he lets his staff vote on his plans. Yes, he does. He says, "All opposed signify by saying 'I resign.' "

11. I used to worry about Harry's opinion of things; then one day he told me he didn't like the equator.

12. He never took a thing that didn't belong to him. We watched him too closely.

13. Look at him: all the warmth and charm of a Southern Sheriff.

14. He surrounded himself with talented and gifted people. Good idea. If you're going to ignore advice, you might as well ignore the best.

15. The only thing you can tell a (job title) is that he's lucky he's not in some other line of work.

16. What a story they told him! It would have broken his heart if he had one.

17. (Name) and (name) were just sitting around . . . out-dulling each other.

18. (Name) couldn't be here tonight; one of his acolytes burned himself on his candle and it was too late to get a replacement.

19. He has a lot of natural talent, but, like his portfolio, it's in someone else's name.

20. He's the kind of guy who wants to have his cake and eat yours too.

21. He has two great assets: he knows the secret of "Winning Friends and Influencing People" . . . and . . . he knows how to keep that secret.

22. Looks good now, doesn't he? Just a month ago he was on the critical list at Weight Watchers.

23. He had so much money he bought four Mercedes: one for each direction.

24. He once called Harry an incompetent and got suspended for eight weeks; one week for slandering Harry and seven weeks for revealing corporate secrets.

25. You can't help admiring him. If you don't, you're fired.

26. Talk about workaholics! I once told him I had worked twelve hours that day and he said a part-time job was better than nothing.

27. Is he in shape? For years we called him Captain Kidd. They both had sunken chests.

28. I think Harry is smarter than Leonardo de Vinci: they say ten people understood Leonardo; nobody understands Harry.

29. He wasn't always this way; it's just that someone once gave him some bad advice; he said "Be Yourself."

30. Misplaced ego? He went to a wedding feast last weekend and tried to get eight serving girls filled with wine so he could turn them into a party.

31. He's not always a yes man. Sometimes when the boss says "no," he says "no," too.

32. Indecisive? I asked him if he could make a decision without delay and he said "yes and no."

33. It's not all his fault. He had a personality bypass.

34. He tries to be classy. Since that business trip to (destination) I notice that when he pulls the tab off his beer cans, he sniffs them.

35. Why are you always dressed like you just ran from a burning building?

36. One morning he came in at 11:00 and (boss) said, "You

should have been here two hours ago." He said, "Why? What happened?"

37. I said "Be objective." He said, "I'm too knowledgeable to be objective."

38. Have you seen his car? He took it to the garage and asked what he should do about it. They told him to jack up the radiator cap and drive a new car under it.

39. He bought his kid a horse and asked the man from the stable if the horse was a thoroughbred. The man said, "Pal, if that horse could talk, he wouldn't speak to you."

40. Did you see his new suit? The jacket fits fine but the pants are too tight across the chest.

41. He asked me what he could wear with a tie like that. I suggested a beard.

42. He's so contrary that if he ever fell into the (river) we'd look for him upstream.

43. His admirers called him a Superman. The only thing he and Superman have in common is that they both take off their clothes in phone booths.

44. Ever since he moved into his "Office of the Future" he's complained about low back pain. Then his secretary found him sitting in the wastebasket.

45. It's not his fault his Bible only had eight commandments.

46. He does look different tonight. Well, in the first place, he's put on a few pounds . . . he put on a few pounds in the second place, too.

47. When they served him his (food) tonight, he called the waiter back and said, "Yes, that's what I want, bring me some."

48. He spends a lot of time at the Louvre staring at the Mona Lisa. She's the last woman in Paris who still smiles at him.

49. Warm human being? He donated blood to the Red

Cross a couple of times before they heard complaints of people freezing up.

50. Will, I heard him admit it. He said he isn't God—his father is.

51. He's been accused of being a ham—not true. A ham can be cured.

52. Harry is ruthlessly efficient. I called him last week for directions to a new restaurant and Harry said: "Highway 495 North for 2.5 miles, take exit 12, then it's 3 miles on your left." I tried to thank him and he said: "No thanks, just repeat the instructions!"

53. What kind of a boss is Harry? One day last winter I came in at 11:00 A.M. and found him sitting in my office waiting for me. I said "Sorry Harry, I fell on the ice coming out my front door." Harry nodded and said: "That took two hours?"

54. I remember the time we went on an outing to the Franklin Park Zoo. Harry went looking for the men's room and wandered by mistake through a back door into the tiger cage. I ran to his wife yelling; "Do something! Harry's in with the tiger!" She looked at me and said, "Why? I don't care what happens to some old tiger."

55. Harry is always looking for the cheapest way out. If you do him a big favor he says: "Thanks a hundred."

56. People ask if Harry and I ever have a difference of opinion. The answer is yes, but I never tell him.

57. Harry likes his people to meditate. He's always saying: "Sit down and shut up!"

58. Good manners and decorum are important business assets, as we all know . . . I guess that's why Harry took etiquette lessons from John McEnroe.

59. We have a street downtown named after Harry. It's called "One Way."

60. Give him an inch and he thinks he's a ruler.

61. You may have noticed that Harry never drinks. I asked him about it once and he said that he never drinks at work and, when he's away from work, he doesn't need to drink.

62. Harry is so square they could build a Vermont village around him.

63. If you are ever looking for Harry, look until you find two guys together and one of them looks bored. The other is Harry.

64. Here's another example of an open mind . . . that probably should be closed for repairs.

65. I don't want to pick on his wardrobe, but he looks like a one-man slum.

66. Harry has a minor speech impediment but it only bothers me when he's giving advice: I can hear him perfectly.

67. He's so straight. He heard that someone was having an affair and he wanted to know who was catering it.

68. I won't comment on his looks, but we hired a photographer to take a corporate portrait of him and the guy refused to develop it. He said he didn't want to be alone in the darkroom with it.

69. Harry says he's on a diet program and goes horseback riding every morning. It's partially successful; so far the horse has lost thirty pounds.

70. I'm on your side, Harry. Some people said you were afraid of your own shadow, and I said, "That's understandable; his shadow looks like a crowd."

71. Harry can't use all his management techniques because the company expressly forbids beatings.

72. People ask how Harry survived all these years anyway. The answer is as plain as his nose in your business.

73. Harry's suits never go out of style. They look like that year after year.

74. I won't pick on Harry's wardrobe, but I do hope he buys himself a new bathing suit this year. The one he wears has a big hole in the knee.

75. Harry really only gets on my nerves twice a year, but it's for six months each time.

76. I think Harry's preoccupation with clothes comes from his childhood days when he had to wear hand-me-downs. His sister was so much bigger that nothing fit right.

77. People shouldn't tell jokes about bald people. They say that God made a lot of heads and those that weren't perfect he covered up with hair.

78. Inside, Harry has the charm of Cary Grant, the humor of Burt Reynolds, the looks of Tom Selleck . . . Harry was just born inside out.

79. Harry went on a crash two-week diet. He lost fourteen days.

80. Harry can be needlessly aggressive. A waitress said, "Have a nice day" and Harry said, "You don't tell me what to do."

81. Harry just doesn't look like an executive. Yesterday at lunch he ordered the Businessman's Special and they asked for identification.

82. Harry's ego still gets him in trouble. At an Engineering Society meeting he introduced a colleague as ". . . the second best engineer in the business." Well, people were offended and we insisted that Harry apologize. So he walked over to the guy and said: "I'm sorry you're the second best engineer in the business."

83. I wouldn't call Harry cheap but his wife asked him for $5. Harry said, "What happened to the $5 I gave you three days ago, Serial # D 785239F?"

84. Harry loves to drive people crazy. He'll send someone a wire saying, "Ignore first wire."

85. But Harry does have a nice even disposition ... miserable all the time.

86. But doesn't Harry look great? That suit fits you like a glove. (pause) Too bad it doesn't fit you like a suit.

87. Sure he's getting bald. It just proves people were right when they said he would come out on top.

88. Harry is involved, he's dedicated, he's committed. (pause) At least he should be.

89. Harry's such a gentleman. He came to work on the subway today, and as a woman was coming into the car, Harry started to get up. She pushed him right back in his seat and said, "I'm a liberated woman and I can stand." A little later he tried to get up and she pushed him back again. Finally, at the third try he said: "Lady, I've been trying to get off for the past two stops; can I go now?"

90. If a laboratory ever studied Harry's chemical makeup, they would find punctuality only as a trace element.

91. (If Harry is short, draw an imaginary line across your waist.) I've had Harry up to here.

92. Friends? Harry has friends he hasn't even used yet.

93. He's the only guy I know who can strut sitting down.

94. Harry knows his capacity. It's just that no matter how hard he tries, he can't make it.

95. Harry started out years ago to find the pot of gold at the end of the rainbow; (looking at Harry) well, at least you found the pot.

96. I don't care what Harry says about his conquests; on his wedding night he was a virgin. I understand that when his bride touched him, he turned his head and coughed.

97. The only time Harry suffers in silence is when he's by himself.

98. What a classy guy. We stopped over his house the other

night and he invited us in to hear some records and have a drink. One of the guys asked him if he had any Rachmaninoff and Harry said, "No vodka, just beer."

99. Harry's idea of a perfect evening is a rare steak, a bottle of Scotch, and a dog. He gives the dog the rare steak.

100. I gave Harry a one-of-a-kind plant for his office: a "Milk of Human Kindness Plant." It blossoms and blooms on love and attention. I'd show it to you, but it died.

101. During the recent economic crunch Harry was so hard pressed for money that he was forced to take some out of his bank.

102. A friend told Harry of a business associate who had passed away and his family gave him an elaborate funeral. "It cost $27,000," his friend said. Harry thought for a moment and said, "Another three grand and they could have buried him in a Mercedes."

103. Now about his style sense: He was going out one day to an important meeting and he asked me if solid blue and blue polka dots could go together. I said yes. So he wore solid blue socks, and a blue polka dot suit.

104. He is stingy with praise. The only way to get yourself congratulated is to tell him what a great manager he is.

105. When you're bald in the front, it means you are a thinker . . . and when you're bald in the back, it means you are sexy. When you are bald in the front and back, it means you just think you're sexy.

106. When Harry came in here tonight, he said: "Oh boy, they've redecorated the bar; put all new drunks around it."

107. Your clothes may be a little loud for others, Harry, but I rather like them. They look like they were designed by the fashion editor of a seed catalogue.

108. Harry's idea of a happy hour is a cup of tea and a nap.

109. I remember going into a bar with Harry one time where we had to step over a guy laying unconscious in front

of the bar. Harry looked down at the guy, then said to the bartender: "Two of those."

110. Harry showed up for work this morning with about the worst hangover I have ever seen. I said, "Harry, why did you get drunk in the first place?" He said, "I don't think I did; I think I got drunk in the last place."

111. Jealous? I told him once I had a car pool and he went out and tried to get one installed in his Mercedes.

112. He was in such a good mood this morning we figured he had seen an accident on the way to work.

113. You can't talk to the man. Today I said, "Harry, don't be so defensive!" He said, "It's not my fault I'm defensive."

114. On beards and mustaches: I never could understand why a man would cultivate on his face what grows wild on his bottom.

115. You look very nice tonight, Harry. . . . and Harry, folks, is not one to get overdressed. In fact, it was just recently we convinced him that "semi formal" does not just mean "best sneakers."

116. Harry is always expensively garbed. You should see some of the expensive garbage he wears.

117. Harry's a sharp dresser in his own way, though. You hardly ever see him when his sweatshirt and sneakers aren't coordinated.

118. What good things can you say about a man who is cheap, bad tempered, and insensitive? Well, I understand he's got a brother who's worse.

119. Harry discovered rather late in life that he was superstitious: he doesn't want to work in any week that has a Monday in it.

120. I don't think Harry is one bit worse today than he ever was. I just think we know him better.

121. Harry really doesn't trust anyone. I remember the day I asked him to be my friend. He said he'd have to discuss it with his attorney.

122. Harry was always outgoing; a high roller. I remember driving to the airport with him and he'd tip at toll booths.

123. I just saw a copy of Harry's personal investment plan: during the '60s he was a bull, during the '70s he was a bear, and during the '80s he's a chicken.

124. Despite what Harry says, he really doesn't want to go. I saw his will and you know how some people leave their bodies to medical science? Well, Harry asked to be stuffed and left in the main lobby.

125. Harry threatened to quit unless the boss let him name his own salary. The boss agreed, so Harry named it "G.D. Lousy Pittance."

126. Harry is so naive that he thinks Masters and Johnson is a golf tournament.

127. Poor Harry just doesn't have much luck with girls. He met this lovely young woman, invited her back to his apartment, and told her to make herself at home. So, she invited her boyfriend over.

128. Harry tried the drinking man's diet. Now he has two problems.

129. One day I was so frustrated I said to him: "Harry, you never listen to me!" He thought for a moment and said, "They say it will rain today."

130. For the first thirty years of our lives, Harry and I never exchanged an unkind word. Then, we met.

131. When you work for Harry, you only have to put in half a day . . . and he doesn't care which twelve hours it is.

132. There's only one way to get in the last word with Harry: apologize.

133. Harry's a "One-Minute Manager." That's not his philosophy or anything; that's just how long he can carry it off.

134. Don't worry about your health, Harry, it will last as long as you do.

135. Waiting for Harry to stop talking can be like waiting for the end of a conveyor belt.

136. But to his credit, Harry can be tolerant of people who disagree with him. He feels everyone is entitled to his own stupid opinion.

137. Some men thirst after riches, some men thirst after success, some men thirst after power. Harry thirsts after peanuts.

138. I remember one meeting that got off on a noisy note and Harry said: "I won't talk until the room settles down!" Somebody in the back yelled: "Go home and sleep it off!"

139. He just doesn't take the time to think. One of the kids asked him: "If the President of the United States died, who'd get the job?" He said: "A Republican undertaker."

140. Harry would never turn someone in need away from his door; he'd let the guy sit there all day if he wanted.

141. When he goes into a bar to get himself a drink, he'll ask everybody, even the bartender; then, if that fails, he buys his own.

142. Harry proved yet again that man is the only animal that can be skinned more than once.

143. Occasionally, though, he has a few absolutely brilliant flashes of total silence.

144. I'd love to be able to drown my troubles; the problem is he puts up such a fight.

145. One of his friends told me about the time he called Harry at his office, and asked how things were going. Harry said, "Just terrific! I'm ahead of all my schedules

and goals, I'm way under budget, and the boss says I'm the most valuable manager the company has!" I asked him what he said then. He said, "I just told him to call me back when whoever was in his office had gone."

146. Harry wasn't ruined by wine, women, or song . . . what did ruin you, Harry?

147. Harry cooked for me just once. He's such a lousy cook, you say grace after you eat.

148. Harry is consistent. You can always count on him to tell the truth about anything that won't hurt him.

149. When we were putting this program together, Harry made one request; that there be no mention of his sex life. He said, "What was, was."

150. Harry has a 2,000-volume personal library . . . all of them autographed copies of his autobiography . . . *My Life as a Sex Symbol.*

151. I asked Harry once if he'd pay $1,000 for a hairpiece; he said no. $500? He said no. $50? He said no. $10? He said maybe if it was a good one. I said, "Gee Harry, you're not very vain." He said, "I am very vain. I like the way I look now."

152. There was a time when Harry would comb his hair to suit existing styles. Now he just styles it to suit existing hair.

153. I remember one party when I told Harry that he'd hate himself the next morning. He said, "That's okay, I'll sleep late."

154. Harry's not such a bad looking guy. Well, I suppose he won't ever make you forget Paul Newman . . . or Edwin Newman, for that matter . . . in fact, he wouldn't make you forget Alfred E. Neuman.

155. There's nothing Harry wouldn't do for me. In fact, he's gone for years and years without doing anything for me.

156. He made his wife get rid of the canary. He was afraid

of catching "Chirpies" . . . someone had told him that was "untweetable."

157. The big spender. He took me out for coffee and donuts one morning . . . it wasn't too bad . . . I just hadn't planned to donate blood that day.

158. Harry's a man who came through the sexual revolution of the '60s without a single enemy contact.

159. Do you know what really frightens me? The thought that someday Harry Gordon will be our nostalgia.

160. Harry bought a Hong Kong suit, and inside the pocket found a note written on the inspector's tag. The note began, "Dear Most Honored Customer," and asked him to send his photograph to a certain address. Harry thought that was nice so he did it. A month later he got a letter from a Hong Kong tailor that read like this: "Thank you for photograph. I have been making these cheap looking suits for many years now and I always wondered what kind of a slob would wear one."

161. Another tip on understanding Harry: When he says "I'm only kidding," he usually isn't.

162. Harry's reputation as a man of innocence is a matter of inspiration to us all. Why he's been found innocent three times in just the past year alone.

163. He seems to wear his clothes forever. The last time he bought a new suit the tailor picked up the old one and asked: "Will you throw it away at home or should I burn it here?"

164. Harry's been a little quieter since we told him his voice was too loud for indoor use.

165. Harry's not cheap. He just has short arms and low pockets.

166. I remember the first time I saw Harry. He was standing on a windy street corner in Chicago . . . wearing a trench coat with the collar turned up . . . his hair blowing in the wind . . . and him too proud to run after it.

167. I saw Harry walking through the corridors without his glasses and asked him if he had purchased contacts. He patted my face and said, "No, this is my way of making new friends."

168. Harry, you just got a call from the Red Cross Blood Bank. Your blood bounced.

169. If Harry were any more religious than he is now, he'd try to wear stained glass contact lenses during Lent.

170. The kind of guy who'd do a good day's work for a good week's pay.

171. Harry is not short. He couldn't afford a face lift, so they lowered his body.

172. Notice Harry taking notes over there so he'll have something to read from when he gets up here. He's not much at ad-libbing. In fact, he can't go in to buy a new suit without a script in his hand.

173. Harry says he read a book the other night that made him cry. But then, card tricks make Harry cry.

174. Harry is written up in the *Guinness Book of Records* . . . under "Lowest Recorded Tippers."

175. I only saw Harry get into a fight once, and it didn't last long. In less than a minute the other guy was down and Harry was begging him to get up. The other guy was on top of Harry at the time.

176. All of us here tonight really enjoy good music, Harry, but later on you can sing anyway.

177. Harry went into a store to buy a new stereo system and the clerk said, "Just give me a small deposit and pay nothing for six months." Harry grabbed him and yelled, "Who told you about me?"

178. Whenever Harry borrows money he borrows more than he needs so he'll have enough to make the first few payments.

179. Harry is not intimidated by expenses. When his Diner's

Club bill gets too high, he just charges it to his American Express.

180. I saw Harry reading a sex manual the other day. It was called: *The Approved Irish Catholic Manual of Acceptable Love-Making Techniques . . . And How to Avoid Them.*

181. Harry's a bit slow at times. Couldn't tell you whether an elevator is going up or down unless you gave him two guesses.

182. Harry is sincerely trying to tone down his aggressive tendencies. The other day he told me about a disagreement he had with (name) and he said, "I changed his mind using only my verbal skills." I said, "That's terrific, Harry, what did you say?" Harry said, "I just told him that if he didn't do it my way, I'd beat him senseless."

183. Harry's staff meetings are two hours worth of emotional interruptions with short breaks to remove the wounded.

184. We all know that people's perception of an issue depends on how it is reported to them. For example, if Harry had been there when the Lord walked upon the water, he would have reported it this way: "Saviour Can't Swim!"

185. Doctor told Harry to give up half his sex life. Poor guy doesn't know whether to give up talking about it or thinking about it.

186. Harry has a firm chin, and lately the firm has taken on a couple of new partners.

187. He's so literal. He went into the Post Office last week for twenty dollars worth of stamps and when the clerk said, "What denomination?", Harry answered, "Catholic."

188. Harry says he's used so much artificial sweetener that

he's artificially fat. Oh well Harry, that's still better than artificial diabetes.

189. Harry's wife saw his shadow last Groundhog Day and predicted six more weeks of dieting.

190. If silence is golden, Harry must own Fort Knox.

191. Harry has a cold. He's been drinking from too many damp glasses.

192. The girls say his lovemaking skills remind them of an intoxicating liquor: Old Grandad.

193. He never forgets anything because when an idea crosses his mind, it's such a very short trip.

194. Harry can get himself into more trouble than a lightning rod salesman caught in the middle of a field, holding a bunch of samples.

195. What happened to your hair, Harry? Looks like some kid from barber school flunked his final on your head.

196. The last party Harry attended, he partied a little too much, went home and fell into a deep sleep. He was still groggy when he got up and didn't come into the office until ten. The boss glared at him. Harry said, "Okay, I'm an hour late!" The boss said, "I don't mind that, but where were you yesterday?"

197. Sometimes Harry's not too classy. He came in here tonight, walked over to the waitress and said, "Hi, toots, I'm the guest of honor, where's the head?" She said, "Go right down that hall and on the left you'll see a door marked 'Gentlemen'; don't mind that, just go right inside."

198. Harry was walking through the airport recently and saw a new machine: a computerized scale. It said, "Your Computerized Weight and Fortune: One Dollar." Well, he had a buck to spare and a minute to kill so he got on, slipped in the dollar, the machine hummed, and out came a note: "Your name is Harry Gordon, you weigh

180 pounds, you are on your way to close an important order." Harry thought that was incredible! He couldn't believe it. He got off the scale, waited a few minutes, got back on and inserted another buck. Out came a note: "Gordon, you still weigh 180 pounds, and if you close this order, you'll be set for the year." Harry still couldn't believe it. He got off, waited a few minutes more, got back on and inserted another buck. Out came this note: "You, Harry Gordon, are the 180-pound idiot who just blew three bucks to miss his plane!"

199. Harry must have a sixth sense; there's certainly no indication of the other five.

200. Harry spent this afternoon down at the barber shop . . . reminiscing.

201. Harry would be the first to admit his faults, if he thought he had any.

202. Harry went home recently and he was met at the airport by the "Harry Gordon Fan Club." He said his mother never looked better.

203. Harry had a complaint in a restaurant once and he pushed his way past a "No Admittance" sign to find the manager. What he found was a German Shepherd attack dog, looking at him eye to eye. Harry screamed for the manager and said, "Is this dog safe?" The manager thought for a moment and answered, "Well, I'd say he was a lot safer than you are."

204. He gave me this tie for Christmas. I said, "Harry, why is it all wet?" He said, "The poor guy didn't have an umbrella over his pushcart."

205. Last Christmas, (name) called and asked if I got the bottle he sent me. I said no and asked him how he had sent it. He said, "With Harry." I said, "That's like sending lettuce leaves with a rabbit!"

206. Harry says he made some money in the market recent-

ly. Sure, he found a pocketbook in the frozen food section.

207. Girls, watch out for Harry. He doesn't have etchings but he might invite you up to see the handwriting on the wall.

208. For a man who is supposed to be artistic, he never knows where to draw the line.

209. Harry has a great memory. He uses it to forget with.

210. I met Harry at the pub one night and bought him a drink. We talked for an hour before he looked at his watch and said, "I was supposed to be home by ten." I said, "Why didn't you say that in the first place?" He said, "I got thrown out of the first place."

211. Just remember folks, Harry's money is tainted! 'Taint yours, and 'taint mine.

212. Harry was so depressed last week; he thought he had varicose veins. He went to the doctor and found out his ballpoint pen had been leaking again.

213. Harry finally got to be important enough to take two hours off for lunch; but now the doctor only lets him have soup and crackers.

214. I remember a while back we had a "Bring Your Own" party. I brought the beer. (Name) brought the snacks. (Name) brought the food. (Name) brought the music. Harry brought his brother.

215. Harry says he dropped forty pounds: On whom?

216. Harry passed a scale on main street, stopped, and put in a nickel. The scale was broken and the needle stopped at 150 pounds. His wife looked at the dial and said, "My God, Harry, you're hollow!"

217. You should see the kinds of places he goes! (Looking around) Trust me, this is the Ritz! He took me to one place; I said, "Nice idea, Harry, sawdust on the floor."

He said, "That's not sawdust, it's yesterday's furniture."

218. He's quite a man, our Harry is. I remember once he made a whole gang of tough guys run: He ran; they ran after him.

219. He went into Saks to buy some perfume as a gift. The clerk said, "This brand is $100 an ounce; it's called 'Perhaps.'" Harry said, "For $100 an ounce I don't want 'Perhaps,' I want 'For Sure.'"

220. Harry invited us to his home last December. It was lovely: a beautifully lighted tree in the front yard, holly around the windows, children singing carols. My wife said, "Oh, look, they're carrying in a yule log!" I said, "Shhh! That's no yule log, that's Harry!"

221. Remember Harry, horse sense is what keeps horses from betting on people.

222. He's not feeling well today. He's had his foot in his mouth so many times that he has athlete's tongue.

223. I'm not saying he's cheap but, when I collected for the (name) fund, I said, "Harry, give until it hurts." He said, "Are you kidding? The very idea hurts!"

224. Harry calls himself a light eater. That means as soon as it's light, he starts eating.

225. Are you Australian, Harry? Someone said you looked like a kangaroo with all the kids at home.

226. If you wanted to see some old world charm and manners, you should have been with us earlier tonight. A woman at the bar dropped her purse and Harry immediately reached down, kicked it toward her, and said, "There you go lady, now it's closer."

227. You can always pick out Harry in a restaurant. He's the one with his back to the check.

228. Harry has a very high success rate with the ladies. High in the sense that it's all in his head.

229. I like that suit, Harry. Harry is always asking me what color suit he should buy. I told him that when God made the butterfly and the hummingbird he used bright and glorious colors, but he made the elephant in basic gray.

230. Harry always said he drank nothing stronger than pop. Well, tonight we've been able to see what "pop" drinks.

231. They say you are what you eat, Harry. Look at him! He's trying to hide that shrimp salad!

232. Harry likes to say: "Okay, so I have a snack at night before I go to bed; is there anything wrong with that?" And we tell him, "Harry, that's what the shark in *Jaws* said just before he ate the boat."

233. When Harry woke up after his operation, he asked the doctor why all the shades were down. The doctor said, "There's a big fire across the street and I didn't want you to think the operation had failed."

234. Chivalry is not dead. Last week on the subway, Harry was seated in front of an old woman who was loaded down with bundles. Harry motioned her over and said, "I get off at the next stop; be alert now and grab my seat!"

235. Weightlifting builds up the chest and shoulder muscles, swimming builds up the arms, running builds up the legs . . . Harry, do you do a lot of horseback riding?

236. Harry's been active in community affairs for years, but so far no one even suspects.

237. I asked him how he liked the ballet. He said, "Instead of making those poor kids dance on their toes, they should just hire taller girls."

238. Those who call him cheap weren't with him on the rainy afternoon that he and I walked through town. Ahead of us was this poor old man whose shoes were so bad, the soles were actually flapping loose. Harry stopped the man, reached into his pocket and pulled out a roll of bills that would choke a horse. He slipped off the rub-

ber band, gave it to the guy and said, "Put this around your shoe to stop the flapping."

239. Harry has broken every watch he has ever owned, so last Christmas his wife bought him an expensive one that was practically indestructible. It was waterproof, shockproof, anti-magnetic, had an unbreakable crystal . . . nothing could possibly break. Harry lost it.

240. Harry's wife was showing the kids their old family album and one of the little guys pointed at a picture and asked, "Who's that good looking guy with the curly hair and the big muscles?" Harry's wife smiled and said, "That's your father dear." The little kid looked over at Harry and asked, "Then, who is he?"

241. He told his wife he had to go in for an examination. He had a love-life problem. He said, "The last time I made love, I broke into a hot sweat, and the time before that, I nearly froze!" His wife said, "That's understandable. The last time was in August and the time before that was February."

242. How about the time he was walking through the woods and he found a little pond where a bunch of girls were skinny dipping. They said, "We won't come out until you leave!" Harry said, "I'm not here to look at you, I just came here to feed the piranha."

243. At his last physical, his doctor said, "This is a personal question Harry, but in the middle years it's important to know. Do you and the wife have any trouble with mutual satisfaction?" Harry says, "No sale doc, we're staying with Prudential."

244. Harry's wife told him, "If you come home late one more night like you did last night, I will pack up and leave you." Sure enough, the next night he was in the same condition and late again. This time he twisted his tie to one side, popped off a few buttons, and came running into her yelling, "Don't pay the ransom, I've escaped."

245. As a boy, he used to study all the torrid love scenes in the movies, until the ushers took his flashlight away.

246. And as for his reputation as a lavish giver of gifts. Well folks, he's known as the "K-Mart Playboy."

247. Harry's cut his drinking in half: he's eliminated the mixers.

248. Harry is not lazy; he has a medical problem. It's called "involuntary inertia."

249. He told her, "Be careful woman, lest you bring out the beast in me." She said, "Who's afraid of mice?"

250. One woman told him that he reminded her of Don Juan . . . as well as others who had been dead for years.

251. Harry has great reflexes. He just can't see a belt without hitting below it.

252. I asked his secretary if she ever went to a psychiatrist. She said, "Only once. He charged me $100 to lie on a couch and answer personal questions. Harry will do that for nothing."

253. Once you really get to know him, you can better appreciate the pleasure of his absence.

254. I must say this for Harry; in his relationships with women he is always frank and earnest. On the East Coast he calls himself "Frank" and on the West Coast he calls himself "Ernest."

255. All of us on your staff owe you a lot Harry—ulcers, hives, nerves, sleeplessness. . .

256. He thinks he has every ailment he reads about. Last week he called his doctor to complain about some disease he saw in National Geographic. The doctor said, "That's ridiculous! In the first place, you wouldn't ever know you had that because there is no pain, discomfort, or indication of any kind." Harry said, "But those are exactly my symptoms!"

257. He was lost once. His parents went to the police with

a photo and said, "Here's our boy, we want to find him." The cop looked at the picture for a while and asked, "Why?"

258. He can be so sarcastic! Like tonight; waiting for dinner, he told the waiter to visit the zoo so he could watch the turtles race by.

259. Abstinence is not Harry's forte. I asked him once if he had ever suffered from delirium tremens. Harry said, "I don't think so, but sometimes it's hard to know where my job ends and the D.T.s begin."

260. I returned to work after that big operation and Harry called me into his office. "What do you think?" he asked. I said, "I'll be all right Harry, but a twelve-hour operation is quite an ordeal." Harry said, "Not about you, you damn hypochondriac, how do you like my new furniture?"

261. Harry was a ghostwriter, but he started playing around too much with the spirits.

262. He tries to be so erudite and cultured. We were walking through a mall the other day and we passed a sculptured bust on display, and Harry said, "That's Shakespeare." "Harry," I said, "it's a music display and that's Mozart." Harry says, "Yeah? Well, that shows how much I know about the Bible."

263. We are not going to make any further remarks about your size Harry. A word to the wide should be sufficient.

264. All this talk about Harry being cheap is really a bum rap. Why, one of his favorite summer pastimes is to sit in his window and throw quarters to the little kids playing in the street. One day he nearly had a stroke when the string broke.

265. Harry is not an ocean traveler. He told his wife that he'd only agree to a cruise if it was on the medical ship "Hope."

266. With all these best-selling diet books on the market, Harry decided to develop and market his own diet plan. It's the "Harry Gordon If-It-Tastes-Good-Spit-It-Out Diet Plan."

267. I hope you all remember that this is Holy Week! No, it has nothing to do with Easter or Passover. We call it Holy Week whenever Harry's in town.

268. Here he is, the originator of the bumper sticker: "Make Love, Not Deadlines," Harry Gordon!

269. Last Halloween we had a big social get-together; cocktails, dinner and dancing, and we all rented costumes. Except for Harry—he just wore one of his old business suits.

270. Harry went to a temperance meeting and this very attractive woman speaker said that if anyone drank a pint of whiskey a day for a year, their stomach would be destroyed. Harry jumped to his feet and said, "I've had a pint a day for a year and more, and I'll put my stomach up against yours anytime!"

271. A high opinion of himself? Last summer at the lake, he went out for a walk and almost got run over by a speedboat.

272. He's the only person I know who'll try to pay off a loan with post-dated cash.

273. Harry still smokes, and if you ask him, he'll tell you about his friend Willard who gave up a three-pack-a-day habit. He stayed off them for four years, and then got run over by a Marlboro truck.

274. Harry's doctor has advised him to give up those cozy little dinners for two. Either that, or get someone to eat with him.

275. In the sixties he used to walk around with a blank picket sign yelling, "This space for rent!"

276. Harry is not a religious man. Sometimes I even think he'd be an atheist if they only had a few more holidays.

277. I'm not saying that Harry likes to straddle the fence on important issues, but the latest joke around the office is: Why did Harry cross the road? To get to the middle!

278. Harry likes to talk about other people. He has a keen sense of rumor.

279. Harry made a new friend tonight. He walked into the bar, sat down, and told the bartender, "I'm a little stiff from tennis." The bartender said, "Welcome pal, I'm from Ohio myself."

280. Harry took a course on memory improvement and it has really helped. Now he can often remember that he has forgotten something.

281. He finally got a woman to invite him up for dinner. Afterwards, she put on a little "not in the mood" music.

282. If you talk to him about a rock group, he thinks you mean Stonehenge.

283. Be very careful when Harry sounds sincere. He only gets sincere when all other forms of deception have failed.

284. Is it possible for one of us to make a fool out of ourselves without knowing it? Not as long as we have Harry Gordon.

285. The only thing Harry ever did on time was to buy a car.

286. Nobody pushes Harry around. Tonight, in the bar, someone called him an obscene name. Harry told him to step outside and say that. The man walked right out the door and said, "How this?" And Harry said, "No good, I can still hear you!"

287. Once after Harry had let out a long stream of profanity, I asked him where he ever learned such language. Harry said, "Learned it, hell, it's a gift!"

288. I like that outfit Harry, what's that around your neck? Wow, talk about the tie that blinds!

289. Let's go easy on Harry tonight. He's given up drinking. He has lived for days on nothing more than food and water.

290. Reverend Harry learned that you don't preach about a fool and his money being parted; at least not until after you take up the collection.

291. People ask why Harry isn't a vice president. Well, he didn't want to peak too early.

292. Harry says he just turned forty. He didn't turn forty, he gutted it.

293. Harry's the kind of gambler who'd drive to Las Vegas in a $25,000 Cadillac, and come home again in a $200,000 Trailways bus.

294. Harry's a relaxed sort of person. He had his portrait painted once and it turned out to be a still life.

295. Harry showed me his wine cellar. I had never seen sparkling Thunderbird before.

9. Service Background

1. His draft board classified him 4-Y. In case of war he's a hostage.

2. I was going to talk tonight about Harry's years in uniform; but then, if you've heard one Boy Scout story, you've heard them all.

3. Anyone who thinks "Old Soldiers Fade Away" never saw Harry trying to get into his old Army uniform.

4. Harry entered the service and learned some valuable things that were to sustain him for the rest of his life. Like . . . big potatoes are easier to peel than small ones.

5. Harry says he could have attended one of the service academies but he was too proud to speak to a congressman.

6. The (Sales VP) told me he was in the Army. I asked "Commission?" and he said, "No, straight salary."

7. He's not exactly a veteran . . . but during the 1960s he did play frisbee for peace.

8. And the Army never drafted him either. He had a Critical Skill: his uncle ran the draft board.

9. As soon as war was declared, Harry was the first guy in town to go to the front . . . window and wave goodbye to our troops.

10. Once Harry and I were talking about the service years and he asked, "Did they put saltpeter in your food way back then?" I said yes and he said, "Me too, and I've only started to notice it lately."

11. Harry loves the Italian people. It was during World War II that an Italian girl hid him from the authorities in her family's cellar until the danger was past. All this happened right here on (name) street.

10. Where Does Subject Consider Home

1. I don't have to tell you (name) is British. If he were any more British, he'd be unintelligible.

2. I said, "Look, you are very lucky to be a German (Japanese, etc.) citizen in today's world. Why would you want to become an American now?" He said, "I want to feel I won World War II."

3. He tried to impress (name) by taking him to a deli for lunch. He ordered two bagels on rye.

4. I can always tell when (name) had spent a few days down home in (Southern State); for the next week, he was virtually unintelligible.

5. I don't want to say his home town is a little backwards, but the mailmen won't wear their gray uniforms anymore. People kept mistaking them for Confederate troops.

6. His father told me that he almost lost Harry as a child . . . thinks now he should have taken Harry further into the woods.

7. Talk about nasty dispositions . . . when Harry was a kid, he had an imaginary friend . . . who wouldn't play with him.

8. Harry's home town was not only small, it was dull. The best cocktail lounge in town was a brown paper bag with a half bottle of Seagrams.

9. They put Velveeta cheese in the gourmet section of the local supermarket.

10. Harry was born in Minneapolis, which was good news for St. Paul.

11. Harry comes from a rural section of the country. The Bridal Suite is a '57 Chevy.

12. Harry, the people back home still carry a torch for you. They've still got the tar and feathers, too.

13. I first met Harry many years ago, and we became friends after I took a thorn out of his paw.

14. New Yorkers are not rude. They just don't want to be mistaken for tourists.

15. Can you imagine a world without New Yorkers? A world without pushing, shoving, and line cutting?

16. Harry's looks have always been against him. He told me once that his father never told him the facts of life because he never thought Harry would have to use them.

17. Harry is going to live forever. The folks in his home town were so healthy, they had to shoot a couple just to get the cemetery going.

18. Harry's family hoped he'd become a doctor when, as a small boy, he tried to start a practice with the little girl next door. Harry gave up when she told him she was a Christian Scientist.

19. Harry comes from a small town, with simple joys. Every Saturday night, he and his buddies would go down to the filling station, stomp on the hose, and listen to the bell ring.

20. Harry says it's rude to ask anyone if they are from Texas. If they are, they will tell you; if they are not, don't embarrass them.

21. Harry says all that place really needed was a little more water and a few more good people. Of course, that's all Hell needs too.

22. He came from a unique little town; and "Unique" is from the Latin "Uni" meaning "One" and "Equus" meaning "Horse."

23. When Harry was promoted to vice president, he called his mother back in (town) and asked if it made the local papers. He said, "I suppose it was the talk of the town." His mother said, "Not really; old man Perkins' barn burned down that same day."

24. I stopped by his home last Thanksgiving Day. It was very nice. He offered standard holiday flare . . . some nuts . . . a few flakes . . . and some other people I didn't know.

25. Harry was the kind of kid who made his parents wish that birth control was retroactive.

26. His hometown is a nice little place. It's just too bad they didn't build it somewhere else where folks could enjoy it.

27. He came from a nice little place, (name). It's sort of like Detroit . . . but without the sparkle.

28. It was at this time that Harry learned that the straight and narrow path was not the one to go to town on.

29. It wasn't easy for Harry, growing up in (city). He used to play hide and seek, and no one would ever look for him.

30. We all know Harry as a middle-aged intellectual. That's anyone over forty who can listen to the *William Tell* Overture without thinking of the Lone Ranger.

31. Harry can speak three languages fluently: Brooklyn, Bronx, and Manhattan.

32. On the army rifle ranges, you could always pick out the

guys from Chicago. After they fired, they wiped their fingerprints off the guns.

12. Personal Interests

1. Someone told him about a man who had beaten his wife to death with a golf club. He asked, "How many strokes?"

2. He likes to sing. One night he gave of his time and sang for some old gentlemen at a nursing home. At the end of the evening he smiled at them and said, "I hope you get better." They said, "You too."

3. I played tennis with Harry just the other day. It was the first time I had ever seen suede tennis balls.

4. He was a founder of Athletics Anonymous: whenever you get an urge to run, jog, or lift weights, they'll send someone over to drink with you until the urge passes.

5. He's trying to get cultured; told me he went to the ballet last week; said he bought $50 seats and still couldn't hear a word they said.

6. He works at his physical conditioning, too. Some days he just goes out and runs ten miles. It may take him all day but he does it.

7. He suffered a lot from being misunderstood; but then, if we understood him better we might have made him suffer more.

8. I knew he was a classy guy the night we went to the little French restaurant and he asked to see the beer list.

9. Harry's wife told me about this holiday costume party they went to all dressed up as a horse. She went as the head and Harry just went as himself.

10. Harry says he's not a real gambler, he just makes bets in his head. That probably explains why he's losing his mind.

11. Is he a sports fan? Harry lives, eats, and sleeps sports! Once on the road he overslept so I called him and said

"Harry, it's twenty to nine!" Harry said: "In whose favor?"

12. Harry used to speak and perform at hospitals all over this area. What a rotten thing to do to people already in pain!

13. Harry likes to brag about how far back in history his family line goes. I got tired of listening once and asked him if he could prove it. "I can't," he said, "Our records were lost during the Great Flood."

14. You know that couch in his office? He calls it "Nautilus." Then he tells people he put in an hour this afternoon on the Nautilus.

15. Harry used to play the violin in local vaudeville shows, but he quit. They used to put him on after the monkey acts and people just thought he was an encore.

16. Harry met his wife on a blind date. Some friends told her to dig up a date . . . . and I guess that's just what she did.

17. Farsighted? Out hunting once I saw him pick up a snake and try to kill a stick with it.

18. Harry is a real nature lover. Isn't that great, considering what nature did to him?

19. Once on a camping trip, a rattlesnake bit Harry on the leg. It was just a horrible experience . . . watching that snake twitch and die.

20. I remember Harry playing golf at the (exclusive club). He took a wicked cut at the ball; it did a perfect 360, and smashed the dining room window. The manager came running out and said, "What are you going to do about that shot?" Harry said, "I think I'll hold my elbows closer to my side."

21. Harry's first book wasn't well received. In fact, the publisher rewrote it before he threw it away.

22. Harry's writing career received another setback recent-

ly when a publisher rejected not only what Harry submitted, but anything he might write in the future.

23. Harry played tennis all afternoon. He won't believe that tennis was invented by a heart surgeon trying to drum up new business.

24. He played a horse the other day that ran so slowly, the jockey kept a diary of the trip.

25. Harry is getting enthusiastic about his exercise program. He told me he was up at 6:30 this morning. He took a brisk walk to the bathroom and was back in bed at 6:35.

26. Harry says he only gambles for laughs. I was with him once when he laughed away his car.

27. Harry did play Little League ball. As a matter of fact, his mother managed the team. I remember during the play-offs, with the bases loaded, he struck out and his mother traded him.

28. Harry recently took up skiing. His instructor tells me he's doing great. He says Harry can now get on the lift without falling off.

29. What a sense of geography! He tells people he likes to vacation along the rockbound shores of Vermont.

30. I remember the time Harry played the piano. The piano lost.

31. Harry says: "Don't call me uncultured. I go to operas, concerts, ballet, all that crap!"

32. The only exercise he gets is from jumping to conclusions.

33. How much of a sports fan is he? When he wants baseball games to last forever, he thinks of sex.

34. He's a musician. He took up the piano because his beer glass kept sliding off the violin.

35. Don't ever play poker with those guys. I was watching a game the other night when I saw a guy slip an ace from the bottom of the deck. I told Harry and he said, "That's okay, it's his deal."

36. Look at him . . . not much of a poker face is he? In fact, when he plays poker with his friends they say that looking at his face is the same as cheating.

37. Exercise is second nature to Harry. Unfortunately, no exercise is first nature to Harry.

38. He worked for many years as an itinerant musician. Then one day tragedy struck; the monkey died.

39. I saw him at the change machine, changing dollar after dollar into silver. I said, "Don't you think you have enough?" He said, "What? Quit while I'm winning?"

40. I can't trust a guy who shuffles his business cards before he gives you one.

41. Harry's whole family believes in exercise and conditioning. You think he's in good shape? You should see his Aunt Rocky.

42. He's very musically inclined. At the age of two, he was already playing on the linoleum.

43. He'll break into song at a moment's notice; of course, if he had the key he wouldn't have to break in.

44. Harry is so defensive about that gas-guzzling sports car he bought! He took it into a fancy garage and had it electronically tuned for a thirty-five percent reduction in fuel consumption! Then he bought a computer-controlled carburetor to save thirty-percent and special spark plugs to save another twenty-percent. Finally, he put on steel-belted radials which they told him would save yet another twenty-five percent in fuel! Well, as he was driving home, the gas tank overflowed.

45. In his early writing days, Harry used to do campaign slogans. His most famous effort: "Reelect Senator Kirby: Integrity Is No Substitute for Experience."

46. Have you ever heard Harry sing? He's got a good voice; it's good for cooling hot soup.

47. Harry is an amateur scuba diver. I am pleased to report that he has sunk lower than anyone else with the firm.

48. One comment about his singing: I went with him once to watch the Patriots play at Schaeffer Stadium. Harry stood up along with forty thousand other people to sing "The Star Spangled Banner" until an usher came over and asked him to keep quiet. He was throwing the crowd off key.

49. Harry is consistent anyway. I called him at home last weekend and his wife said he was out back, beating a rose bush into bloom.

50. Harry took a midwinter vacation and went to Las Vegas. He got tanned and faded at the same time.

51. Harry told his caddy, "I bet there are people worse at golf than I am," and the kid said, "Probably, but they don't play."

52. The only problem with Harry's golf game is that he stands too close to the ball . . . after he's hit it.

53. Harry told one of the guys at the club: "My doctor says I can't play tennis anymore" and the guy says: "Oh, he's played with you, too?"

54. After Harry tees off, you don't have to replace the turf, you have to returf the place.

55. One Saturday, he watched me change the air filter in my car and he said, "You know, I've never understood how the air got from there, all the way down to the tires." That's all right, one other time he asked me to help tighten the buckle on the fan belt.

56. He went skiing in Switzerland, got separated from his group, and fell into a deep ravine. He called for help until someone called back. "We're from the Red Cross." Harry yelled, "I gave at work!"

57. His size is interfering a little bit with his golf game. When he puts the ball where he can see it, he can't reach it. When he puts it where he can reach it, he can't see it.

58. The only problem with Harry's golf game is that he stands too close to the ball after he hits it.

59. Harry loves movies, especially gangster movies; goes to as many as he can. I think he just likes to be with his own kind.

13. Subject's Personal/Business Philosophy

1. He learned that (integrity, punctuality, etc.) is a virtue . . . . if you don't mind being lonely.

2. He's a profound thinker. He wonders about things like: Is Darwin's birthday a religious holiday for apes?

3. Many a wise word has been spoken in jest, Harry, but for sheer volume they can't compare with the number of stupid words you've spoken in earnest.

4. Robber barons made money the old-fashioned way . . . they stole it.

5. He won't go to an X-rated movie. He can't stand the idea of seeing someone have more fun in ninety minutes than he's had in his entire life.

6. His motto: Start the Day with a Smile . . . and Get It Over Early.

7. He's written his memoirs. They were purchased by Parker Brothers and will be released next year as a game.

8. Harry's philosophy speaks to the ages . . . the ages between eight and fourteen.

9. We've had to watch Harry's public speaking engagements ever since he alienated the Sequoia Club; they asked for suggestions on saving trees and Harry said they should shoot woodpeckers.

10. Poor Harry! He finally got it all together, and then he forgot where he left it.

11. Harry has a number of little mottos to live by like: Always be sincere, even if you have to fake it.

12. Talk about a big heart. If you walk up to Harry with a sad story and ask him for anything, out comes his

wallet and he'll show you a picture of (Company President).

13. Harry has *Playboy* in his briefcase. He reads it for the same reason he reads *National Geographic;* to see places he'll never get to visit.

14. He's an honest man though. On his last 1040 he reported half his salary under "Unearned Income."

15. Harry's a clergyman of sorts. Some comfort the afflicted. He afflicts the comfortable.

16. Harry is a man of unresolved conflicts. Every day he has to choose between "Have a Nice Day," and "Watch Out for Number One."

17. Getting instructions from Harry is like buying one of those English bicycles. After he goes away, you have to do a lot of assembly.

18. Harry is so cautious, he won't even burn the candle at one end.

19. A few years ago, Harry was quite ill and his wife had the family clergyman visit him in the hospital. "Harry," the clergyman says, "Do you renounce the devil?" Harry, ever the businessman said, "Please, this isn't the time to alienate anyone."

20. You have to admire the way Harry can take a firm neutral stand on every important issue.

21. Harry doesn't enjoy jokes with double meanings . . . because he doesn't get either one of them.

22. Harry always takes advantage of a situation. The other night I introduced him to a personal friend of mine who is a doctor, and Harry started asking him health questions. The poor guy said, "Sorry, I'm not an M.D., I'm a Doctor of Philosophy." Harry thought for a minute and said: "Okay, then what is the meaning of life?"

23. Harry selected his epitaph: "Here Lies a Lawyer and an Honest Man." Who will be in there with you, Harry?

24. Harry told one of the guys that if there is reincarnation next time he's coming back as a tough, insensitive, do-it-my-way kind of manager. Harry, you can't be the same thing twice!

25. Of course you know that Harry's ethnic background is Irish. And maybe he gets his compassion from his Uncle Tim. Uncle Tim staggered home from the pub one stormy night and in the confusion of the drink and the rain and sleet and lightning, he fell into a construction hole. Tim yelled, "Get me a Rabbi!" Some good Samaritan brought a Rabbi and Tim requested the last rites. The Rabbi said, "It's obvious you're a Catholic, why did you call for me?" Tim replied, "You think I'd call a Priest out on a night like this?"

26. But Harry is insightful. The other day, watching a well dressed man step unto a chauffeur-driven limousine, I heard him mutter: "There but for me go I."

27. I asked Harry if he thought he was conceited. He said: "No, I just have a high opinion of people with good looks, personality, and talent."

28. Harry is to (name or organization) what the Med-Fly is to the California fruit growers.

29. Getting business advice from Harry is like getting a kidney transplant from a bed-wetter.

30. You know a guy's got a problem when you hear a remark like this: On our way to the track one day, Harry said to me, "I hope I break even. I need the money."

31. Harry said something to me the other day that is so profound I'd like to share it with you. He said: "Money can't buy friendship, but you get a better class of enemies."

32. If Moses had known him, there could conceivably have been another commandment.

33. Harry feels strongly that privileges bring responsibilities. Ever since we put in the dental plan, he won't let us snarl at him.

34. Harry and his partner proved that although blood may be thicker than water, stock is thicker than both.

35. Harry says he was ruined by wine, women, and song. Apparently, he never had any of them.

36. I remember asking Harry one time to look up the author of all his little sayings. He said, "How do you do that?" So I told him to look in the back of wherever he read it. He came back and said he couldn't find the guy's name, but his initials were B.V.D.

37. If it weren't for T-shirts and bumper stickers, Harry wouldn't have any philosophy at all.

38. Another example of Harry's business philosophy: We'll use our hands and hearts, and, if we must, we'll use our heads.

39. Harry has such a realistic business philosophy. Try this one: All preparation and skill are in vain if the angel of darkness wets on the flintlock of your rifle.

40. Harry agrees with Mark Twain that "Water, taken in moderation, cannot hurt you."

41. If two negatives really make a positive, every second thing he says must be a compliment.

42. Harry's background from the '60s has made him totally nonviolent. Once on a trip, I saw him go into a cocktail lounge, have a few drinks, and then loudly announce: "I can passively resist any man in the house!"

43. As Harry says: "You can't learn anything from history. It's just the same damn thing over and over again."

44. Don't try to teach pigs to sing. You not only waste your time, but you aggravate the pig.

45. His motto: Lousy Salesmen Have Skinny Kids.

46. Harry, you can be so negative. Why don't you take the back of a postage stamp and write down everything you believe in?

47. Harry believes that you can get more out of your peo-

ple with a kind word and a whip than you can with a kind word alone.

48. The American Consumer. The only reason folks aren't buying more elephants is that no one offers them on a time payment plan.

49. He was arguing with (name) over whether his business plan was based on the thinking of Sloan of GM, Rockefeller of Standard Oil, or Morgan of US Steel. (Name) said, "Easy, let's open their graves and see which one is spinning."

50. After speed-reading the Bible, Harry came away believing Joan of Arc was Noah's wife.

51. The only religious thing I saw him do was to refuse to work on the Sabbath.

52. He believes, with Lincoln, that you can fool some of the people all of the time, and all of the people some of the time. He thinks that's usually enough.

53. He knows what makes people tick. Did you see his note on the bulletin board? "The terminations will continue until morale improves."

54. It was he who first had the idea of taking the pins out of the map and sticking them into the salesman.

55. He's an old line manager and has trouble with certain modern concepts. Like: How can a plane which travels at over 700 m.p.h. always be late?

56. His version of "cold sales call" is just a step above "breaking and entering."

57. He's always thinking of business. A tramp told him he was dying of exposure and (name) said, "Have your broker cover it at market."

58. He covers an issue the way a screen covers a window: millions of little holes.

59. He was always faithful to his trust. He is not required to divulge the name of his trust.

60. Harry was always the perfect optimist. Somebody asked him how his business had been affected by the recession. Harry said: "... wasn't affected at all! But I will admit it was the lousiest boom year we ever had ..."

61. Harry's integrity of character is another facet of his personality to be admired. He told me once that he attributes all of his success to honesty and wisdom. The honesty to stick to any promise he ever makes regardless of the consequences, and the wisdom to never make a promise.

62. Harry thinks that true beauty comes from within .... within banks, within brokerage firms, and with inside information.

63. A company without a law department is like a fish without a bicycle.

64. Do you remember Harry's "Four-Point Program" to put us over the top last year? When he explained it to us, I mentioned to (name) that I had only heard three points. (Name) said: "The fourth is under his hat."

65. Harry thinks a "naturalist" is a guy who always throws "sevens."

66. Let's get on with the program, and, as Harry would say, "That's only a suggestion, but let's remember who's making it."

67. Harry has a strong sense of righteousness and he was outraged the other day when someone gave him Canadian coins in change. He said: "That's just not fair! I would have been out twenty percent on my money! Why, if that old guy at the newsstand wasn't so farsighted, I probably never would have gotten rid of them!"

68. Harry is to management what bumper stickers are to philosophy.

69. Harry says the difference between genius and talent is that talent gets a weekly paycheck.

70. I like the warm way Harry greets you when you walk into his office: "Well, how do you justify taking up my time?"

71. I suppose that's better than what he used to say: "How can I service you (as we used to say on the farm)?"

72. Occasionally, Harry will offer me a few words of advice. By the way, his "few words" are now available on long-playing records and tapes.

73. We wanted to put a bronze statue of you in the lobby, Harry, but they said it wouldn't stand up with one foot on the ground and one in the mouth.

74. I remember the time Harry told me that he had cancelled all his personal life insurance. He said that when he went, he wanted everyone to be really sad.

75. Harry won't say how much personal insurance he carries, but I do know that when he goes . . . Prudential goes!

76. Harry says you can get more with a kind word and a whip than you can with a kind word alone.

77. Harry makes money. He says he has enough money to meet obligations he wouldn't have if he didn't make so much money.

78. He's the sort of pseudo-intellectual you can ask, "How are you?" and he asks, "Relative to what?"

79. Someone once asked him to be a Jehovah's Witness. Harry said, "Talk to my lawyer; I didn't even see the accident."

80. Harry knows money isn't everything. He knows you can have as much fun with nine-hundred thousand as you can with a million.

81. Harry can draw a mathematically precise line from an unwarranted assumption to an erroneous conclusion.

82. There are two different things that bother me about Harry. He has two different views on nearly every sub-

ject he has to consider; and he sees both sides of an issue so clearly that he can never come to a decision.

83. Harry refuses to let his decision-making process become inhibited by factual considerations.

84. Harry is a gentleman, of strong religious convictions, who is always willing to share his beliefs with us. He reminds me of St. Paul, one of the most boring towns in America.

85. As Harry likes to say, it is better to have loved a short girl than never to have loved a tall.

86. Harry doesn't say much. Sometimes I think he just opens his mouth once in a while to change feet.

87. Harry believes, with the Bible, that it is "... better to give than to receive ... " I just never realized they were talking about advice.

88. I came in here tonight and saw Harry sitting there with a drink, a cigar, and a beautiful woman; and I thought how right you were Harry, when you said: "Cultivate vices while you're young and they won't desert you when you're old."

14. Subject's Proudest Achievement

1. He told (name) that the Book-of-the-Month Club offered him a contract. (Name) said, "Turn it down, you can't write a book each month!"

2. He opened up a tall men's shop—in Tokyo.

3. I believe you can sum up Harry's successful career and all his other accomplishments as well in one perfect word: Luck.

4. I used to say that someday Harry would make it big ... and I still say that someday Harry will make it big.

5. Harry, if it is true that you profit from your mistakes, you are on the verge of a banner year.

6. Harry's name has finally become a household word; but only within his household.

7. How well does Harry sing? Well enough to add a little more grief to the average funeral.

8. He once sang at a club in the tough end of town and they held him over . . . over the side of a bridge.

9. Harry's got good judgment and he says he got it from experience. Of course, he got the experience from bad judgment.

10. Harry told us about the night he was awakened after midnight by a ringing phone only to find a drunk on the other end who wanted Harry to explain his book. Harry said: "Call be back around noon and I'll explain it to you." The drunk said: "Around noon, I won't care."

11. Harry was recently deposed for a company legal action and when they asked his position he said he was the greatest (title) in the world today. Later I asked him why he said that. He answered. "I had to, I was under oath."

12. We wanted to get something for you, Harry, but no one would start the bidding.

13. (Award) When we heard you were leaving, Harry, we decided to present you with something appropriate; something reminiscent of you, the person. We decided on this watch. Why? Well, to begin with, it's an old watch . . . been banged around a few times . . . has to be wound up every morning, and still runs a half hour late all day . . . and then stops working completely somewhere around 5:00 P.M.

14. When we heard you were leaving, Harry, we all decided to get together and give you a little momentum . . . I mean memento.

15. Harry spoke at so many dinner meetings that he used to brag that he'd open his mouth, put in a dinner, and out would come a speech. As for his audience, well, they'd

hear Harry's speech, open their mouths, and out would come dinner.

16. And now, we are pleased to present you with this 1985 Cadillac . . . windshield-wiper blade.

17. Harry received another award recently when he was elected to Who's Through in America.

18. Harry says he is a self-made man. That takes a load of guilt off the rest of us.

19. Well, money hasn't changed you that much, Harry. It's made you proud where we used to say arrogant, outspoken where we used to say rude, and eccentric where we used to say crazy.

III. ASSAULTS AND ZAPPERS

1. I asked him what he had done with all his money. He said that part had gone for booze, part for gambling, part on women . . . and the rest he had spent foolishly.

2. When he's on vacation, he pays one of the kids five bucks a day to wake him up yelling "(Boss) wants to see you—*now!*" Then he says, "Tell (Boss) to go to hell."

3. Someone accused him of being unfaithful. Nonsense, he's been faithful dozens of times.

4. His lectures (sermons) are like the Peace of God; they surpass all understanding.

5. As an objective outsider, what do you think of the human race?

6. There was an earthquake near the bar he was in. He was thrown to his feet.

7. I figured the tobacco lobby had got to him the day he told me M&Ms cause emphysema.

8. He has more business and sales savvy in his little finger than he has in his whole hand.

9. You ought to hear his side of the story . . . provided you can understand him.

10. Ask him about the time he gave blood to the Red Cross and they used it to sterilize their instruments.

11. As a concerned human being he left his brain to Harvard Medical School . . . they are contesting the will.

12. (Subordinate who follows boss around) almost didn't make it tonight either. (Boss) stopped in the corridor today without signaling and (subordinate) was injured in the crash.

13. The Bad News Is: Without a stitch of clothing on, he streaked the (city) Flower Show. The Good News Is: He won first prize for the Best Dried Arrangement.

14. He reads *Penthouse* for the same reason he reads *National Geographic*: to see places he'll never get to visit.

15. That's as bad as the (name of department). They took a popularity poll and no one won.

16. He has a mind like the Rio Grande: wide, dirty, and shallow.

17. A man like him is hard to find. To find him tonight, we had to look in three bars and a massage parlor.

18. He's the kind of guy who gives failure a bad name.

19. He has delusions of adequacy.

20. He has a mind like concrete . . . all mixed up and permanently set.

21. You should have seen him the morning after the last get-together: He looked like a vampire who had just started working days.

22. (After gambling) I hope the casino has more luck with my money than I did.

23. When we were on the boat ride, I offered to get him lunch. He told me to throw it over the side and save time.

24. He writes what he calls "Evening Checks"; they're only good when the banks are closed.

25. You've heard of Miss America and Miss Universe? She was Miscellaneous.

26. You want to know the secret of coming out of a casino with a small fortune? Go in with a big fortune.

27. I stopped at the (local pub) the other night and a pink elephant, an orange snake, and some crazy looking birds walked up to the bar. The bartender said, "You guys are early tonight; Harry isn't here yet."

28. (About two people always seen together) Is anything wrong with (#2)? I saw (#1) in the corridor today and he was alone.

29. (Same as #28) I'm just sorry (#2) couldn't be here tonight . . . he was injured in a slight accident; (#1) stopped at the coffee machine without signaling and (#2) rear-ended him.

30. (Same as #28) I asked (#1) how he felt when (#2) went on vacation. He said: " . . . like somebody shot my dog."

31. And his house . . . it had more mortgages on it than paint.

32. I still don't know if he has a morbid sense of humor . . . or is just cheap. Like the time he put unbreakable glass in the fire alarm boxes.

33. If someone falls into the (fountain, local river, pond) you don't have to worry about his drowning—he'll be poisoned first.

34. On the cruise the other night, he asked to be lashed to the bar.

35. That's not a gleam in his eyes, girls; it's just the light reflecting off his contact lenses.

36. Well regarded? Why he has friends he hasn't even used yet.

37. I don't know what makes him tick, but I hope it's a bomb.

38. I couldn't warm up to him if we were cremated together.

39. He's the only guy I know who can strut sitting down.

40. Bachelorhood is a family tradition among his people. He's a bachelor . . . his father was a bachelor . . .

41. And he's so trusting; some people say he has faith in fools, others call it self-confidence.

42. He used to play football and wore one of those numbered shirts. You know, the ones with your I.Q. on them.

43. Nobody can fault us on our planning. We have one-story buildings so no one can get hurt going off the roof.

44. He's so rich, he has Swiss money in American banks.

45. He gave me a lovely gift last Christmas; a picture for our living room. The picture is called "January." You tear off a piece of paper and there's another picture called "February."

46. He's going to live to be an unknown.

47. People ask us: "How's Harry?" We say, "Compared to what?"

48. As you drive down the highway of business life, you'll find the things that annoy you aren't the ups and downs, the fits and starts, the ins and outs; what's really annoying are (looking around) . . . the jerks.

49. For those of you who like to read mysteries in bed, I'll distribute some of Harry's old memos.

50. The stork that brought you should have been arrested for smuggling dope.

51. Harry ordered the wine for dinner. It was so cheap the restaurant would serve it only in a brown paper bag.

52. I won't say Harry is a chronic complainer, but after

dinner the waiter asked him: "Sir, was anything all right?"

53. Harry tried to have his face lifted once . . . but the crane broke.

54. You have a great head on your shoulders Harry . . . just too bad you never got a neck.

55. Harry wants a convertible but he won't buy one until he can get a toupée with a flesh-colored chin strap.

56. Harry's the kind of guy you'd like to run into . . . but he never walks anywhere you could bring a car.

57. One thing you have to say about Harry: He can put two and two together . . . whether they belong together or not.

58. Harry hosted a cocktail party for us once, and paid for everything out of his own pocket. The whiskey flowed like molasses.

59. I'm glad you picked a nice, trusting place like this. I tried to charge a couple of drinks at the bar and they asked for a cosigner.

60. Harry is so cheap, he asked for separate checks at his wedding reception.

61. Does Harry appreciate a favor? Does he remember it? I'll say he does . . . next time he needs another favor!

62. Harry's wife showed me that beautiful diamond ring he bought her. I told her how marvelous it was and she said, "Yes, it's beautiful, but it comes with the Gordon Curse." I said, "The Gordon Curse . . . what's that?" She said, "Harry Gordon."

63. Harry has trouble with words. He would have resigned years ago if he could spell it.

64. Harry is finally overcoming all those guilt hang-ups he has carried with him for years. He just threw away his old marriage manual: *Sex Without Fun*.

65. Watch Harry at the end of dinner tonight. I don't mind a guy who takes home a doggie bag, but he's got plastic wrap in his pockets so he can bring home the soup.

66. The recession didn't bother Harry. He lost everything during the boom.

67. This is a nice place. I wish Harry would have our offices redecorated. The graffiti on the rest room walls is about the Kaiser.

68. You've got to be compassionate when you realize that Harry has a face that's only good once a year: Halloween.

69. Harry was one of the first men allowed in the delivery room with his wife. Finally the screaming got too bad. The doctor slapped his face and threw him out.

70. Before Harry went into the service he said, "Before I go to War, I want three days of Joy." Then he introduced me to Joy.

71. Harry likes to drive his wife crazy. He doesn't talk in his sleep—he just grins.

72. Harry is quite a reader. He has over 250 books. But he doesn't know where to put them. Nobody will *lend* him a bookcase.

73. Harry's wife went to a psychiatrist about Harry. She said, "I think Harry thinks he's a refrigerator." The doctor said, "That's not such a harmful complex." She said, "Maybe not, but he sleeps with his mouth open and the light keeps me awake."

74. We used to double date. I remember overhearing Harry in the back seat at a drive-in once. He said, "I love you terribly." She said, "You certainly do."

75. I won't say Harry is inconsistent, but the other night he went to an Italian movie, drove home in his Japanese car, poured himself a cup of Colombian coffee into an English bone china cup, sat down on his Danish fur-

niture, ate a French croissant, then picked up a ball point pen made in Taiwan, and wrote to his congressman demanding a stop to the flow of gold out of this country.

76. He tried for years to be a financial success. Harry has an uncanny talent for taking a bankroll and running it into a shoestring.

77. Harry has never said an unkind word about anyone. That's because he never talks about anyone but himself.

78. Harry considered the purchase of some intelligent terminals, but during the demo, he questioned their intelligence because unlike his staff, they didn't listen and nod when he spoke.

79. But Harry knows how to face the music (pause) as long as he can call the tune.

80. And popular; why remember when Harry was in the hospital? He got tons of get-well cards (pause) from the nurses.

81. You'll have to excuse Harry. He got up on the wrong side of the floor this morning.

82. But Harry has done a lot of good for many people. Think of all the people he has kept working for years; bill collectors and IRS agents, to name but a few.

83. In the world of business, Harry is the epitome of efficiency. His files were becoming overcrowded. Harry's secretary suggested destroying all correspondence over six years old. Harry said, "Go ahead, just be sure to make copies."

84. If I can believe only half of the things that have been said here this evening about my friend Harry, then the only thing he has left to look forward to is a cool spot in Hell.

85. Harry is a compassionate man. He visited one of his best friends in the hospital. The doctor had given his

friend six months to live. Harry brought him a calendar.

86. Harry went on the wagon once. He said it was the most boring ten minutes of his life.

87. I don't want to say how much alcohol Harry consumes, but once at (local pub) (a friend) gave him a hot foot and Harry burned for three days.

88. Harry has some venture capital things going for him, though. I understand he has two chinchillas in heat.

89. Investments are not Harry's strong suit. He recently bought an antique automobile . . . a 1926 Toyota.

90. Whenever I think of Harry, two things immediately come to mind—talent and humility. (Pause) Two things Harry has never possessed.

91. Do you know how the man who invented slow motion pictures got his idea? One day he watched Harry reaching for a restaurant check.

92. Now take (name of well respected dais member), for example. Take away his charm, dignity, and class and what have you got? Harry Gordon!

93. I haven't seen Harry in some time. It's good to see him. I told him, "Harry, you look good." He said, "I'm not feeling myself." I said, "Well, that's an improvement in itself."

94. Let's face it; Harry is a warped puck in the hockey game of life.

95. I think it's great that after ____ years of marriage, they have a glass of wine at bedtime. I know that only because I overheard Harry's wife say she goes to bed every night with a cold duck.

96. The other day I accused Harry of being affected and pretentious. He said, "Affected! Pretentious? Who's affected? Moi?"

97. You know, Harry, everyone likes talented, charming,

witty people. But that doesn't mean we don't like you just because you're none of those things.

98. He started out as a poor slob, and I can attest to the fact that success hasn't changed him.

99. He wanted to save himself the trouble of going on a diet, and still wanted to look thin, so he started to hang out with fat people.

100. Harry didn't want to come here tonight but I spoke to him for a while and convinced him to see things my way (some days it's easier to convince Harry than on other days, but it's never difficult).

101. Harry, I've done more for you than your mother did. She only carried you for nine months.

102. Harry's day started off badly as well. He went in for a haircut and right in the middle of it, he slipped off the pony.

103. Asking (name) what he thinks about Harry is like asking a lamppost what it thinks about dogs.

104. Harry bought one of those European cut bathing suits and it was suggested that he stuff a lemon inside to fill it out. "I can't understand what's wrong," he said, "people take one look at me and walk away!" I said, "Harry, why don't you try stuffing it down the front?"

105. Harry's a loner. He prefers his own company. Well, there is no accounting for taste.

106. Harry's such an actor. Ever since Barry Fitzgerald passed away, Harry's tried to play the role of a kindly old Irish Priest.

107. Harry and (friend) are so much alike. They look alike, they think alike, they even dress alike. One day I asked (name) if he thought somebody's daddy jumped the fence way back when. He thought about that for a moment and said: "Impossible! Then only one of them would be a bastard!"

108. Harry's life has been full of trials but, as yet, not a single conviction.

109. Harry's very grateful that we no longer sacrifice the bearer of bad news. His life would be in jeopardy at the end of each fiscal quarter.

110. I think Harry plans to "take it with him." He just bought a fireproof money belt.

111. Harry believes in reincarnation ever since he heard that George Washington came back as a bridge.

112. I'm the best friend he has and I don't like him much.

113. Harry was in analysis for years but he says it was worth it. Now he gets rejected by a better class of people.

114. I can tell it must be near Easter. You all look like you've just come back from the dead.

115. The things Harry will do for his friends can be counted on his little finger.

116. We've been friends for ten years and there's nothing Harry wouldn't do for me. And that's about what he has done for me: nothing.

117. A goose tried to walk through that department once and he was "peopled" six times.

118. The diamond is the hardest object in the world . . . as Harry learned when he tried to get one back.

119. How important is a work station? What is a sarong but a towel that found an interesting place to work?

120. We call it "The Gabby Hayes Project." We call it that because it was started when Gabby Hayes was a very little boy.

121. You all look like the second day of a Hell's Angels' Weekend Picnic.

122. Did you ever see those people? They look like a road company cast from Hair (Evita? Annie?)?

123. He was a consultant, which, as we all know, is a guy between jobs.

124. He's afraid of flying and poison. In both cases, he says, one drop can kill.

125. And she left him because "her feelings had changed." Harry asked for the ring back. She said her feelings hadn't changed about the ring.

126. Nobody understood Harry until (name) came along . . . and he misunderstood Harry.

127. Someone asked me to describe his drinking habits. I said "He seldom buys."

128. He confuses an open mind with a vacant mind.

129. He used to go out and have a drink with some employees. Not employees from here; he hired a few guys of his own to drink with him.

130. He gave up drinking several years ago for the sake of the wife and the kidneys.

131. There he is: every other inch a gentleman.

132. Let's go easy on him tonight. His personal computer broke down this afternoon and he had to do his own thinking.

133. He's dealing with a classier bunch of customers and once in a while he has a problem. The President of the (name) Bank told him about his daughter's coming out party and Harry asked him what she was in for.

134. When they decided to set up a new division, Harry wanted to call it "(product) R Us."

135. He's on a yogurt diet . . . but we don't begrudge him culture in any form.

136. He's not a drinker. His house is so dry you have to prime your mouth before you can spit.

137. They are a tough bunch. It takes three of them to

change a light bulb: one to change the bulb, and two to take care of the witnesses.

138. He gave us a great deal of trouble. It was all he ever gave us.

139. It was the only major American corporation I knew of that hired its operating executives through Office Temporaries.

140. He dieted on and off for twenty-three years. Lost 612 pounds. He should be on a cuff link.

141. He was in a rage that day; his shoe laces weren't the same length on both sides.

142. The last time he was presented with a Loving Cup, his wife burst into uncontrollable laughter.

143. I suppose it had to happen, and one day last year it did: One of his employees met him in the parking lot . . . and hit him. The judge fined the guy $110. The extra $10 was an entertainment tax.

144. Harry put his money into the stock market, where some are bulls, some are bears, and most are goats.

145. And is he a lady killer? Not too many of us know that Harry is the author of that best selling book: *How to Pick Up Desperate Women.*

146. Speaking of being defensive, I understand that Harry gave his wife a mink coat for her birthday. She took it out of the box and said: "Who'd have thought such a beautiful fur could come from some beady-eyed, nasty-tempered little ferret." Harry said. "Well, at least you could thank me!"

147. Harry went in for a physical recently, and his wife went with him. While Harry was dressing, the doctor said to his wife: "I don't like the looks of him." His wife shrugged and said: "He's good to the kids."

148. A little later tonight we'll have Harry demonstrate his expertise in speaking French for you. We'll have him

tell you about the time he ordered from a French menu and the waiter had to tell him he had just ordered "All the above are complete dinners."

149. He's getting better with his French though. Among the things he can say perfectly is: "Give him the check."

150. Harry comes from a very old American family. His ancestors went west in covered wagons. If you could see pictures of his ancestors, you'd know why the wagons were covered.

151. Harry's very proud about coming from a very old family with roots that go back deep into the past. His family history comes in five volumes, and America isn't even discovered until the end of Volume III.

152. If what you don't know won't hurt you, Harry must be damned close to invulnerable.

153. Harry's a very observant kind of guy. The other day he told me that if you walk through the executive area and look into the offices in a certain sequence, you get a pretty good idea of evolution.

154. Sometimes Harry tries to impress people in his office by giving his secretary important-sounding instructions. One day last week he told her: "As soon as this meeting is over, I want you to call my broker," and she answered, "Stock or pawn?"

155. Harry's romantic spirit was crushed years ago when a young woman told him he reminded her of the ocean. "Oh," said Harry, "you mean I'm restless, untamed, and romantic?" "No," she answered, "you just make me sick."

156. Harry has brought us unprecedented growth and expansion! To cite just one example, when he started here he had a boyish figure . . . and he's damn near doubled that, too!

157. Harry did spend a little time in the hospital this year,

but he's fine now. The doctor discharged him after he found Harry trying to blow the foam off his medicine.

158. Such a classy guy! Into all the finer things! He went shopping for a bedroom set and they showed him one in Louis XIV. He said: "I need something bigger; what do you have in Louis XV?"

159. The last time Harry went for a physical, his hands were shaking so badly the doctor asked: "Are you drinking a lot?" Harry said: "No, I spill most of it."

160. Harry called me in last week and said he'd recently heard that after our last big meeting, I was seen pushing a wheelbarrow through the hotel lobby at 3:00 A.M. "Don't you understand," he told me, "that such behavior causes our firm to lose prestige in the public eye? Why would you do such a thing?" "Harry," I told him, "it was the only way I could get you back to your room!"

161. Harry is one of those rare managers who approaches every new subject with an open mouth.

162. We all know Harry led a tough life. Last time he was in church, the Priest was yelling: "You must all pay the price of your sins!" Then he spotted Harry and added: "If you have already paid, please disregard this notice."

163. Harry always had plenty of money. In fact, he once said that his big problem in life wasn't making money so much as it was passing money.

164. I know we are all brothers under the skin, but Harry seems to get under my skin more than most.

165. Harry, if it's true we can learn from our mistakes, you've got a shot at being Manager of the Century.

166. Did you ever see Harry at a computer terminal? The bad news is he can only type with two fingers. The good news is he can still type faster than he thinks.

167. Harry's bachelor lines were never too successful; like

asking girls for their phone numbers because he was writing a telephone book.

168. Admitting you made a mistake to Harry was like cutting yourself in front of Dracula.

169. Anybody who thinks Harry has run out of gas should go out with him some night for Mexican food.

170. It was Harry who first said: "If God wanted me to fly Tourist class, He would have made me narrower."

171. Harry has what they call Saloon Arthritis; every night he gets stiff in a different joint.

172. Harry's such a world traveler. Once he told me: "If you've seen one pyramid, you've seen them all."

173. In his worldwide travels, Harry learned the two secrets of international communications: (1) Everybody else is really speaking English, they just pronounce it poorly; and (2) Anyone will understand Harry if he just speaks loudly enough.

174. Harry is so conservative; if they ever made a movie of his life, it would be filmed by 18th Century Fox.

175. You say he's not too bright? He has to move his lips when he listens!

176. He gets everything backwards; doesn't know his navel from a hole in the ground.

177. He never knighted anyone. Who'd kneel down in front of Harry when he had a sword in his hands?

178. There are three ways to handle Harry. Unfortunately, none of us know what they are.

179. At a big conference like this you can tell a guy's profession by watching him get introduced to a pretty girl. The Manufacturing guys shake hands, the Engineering guys may kiss her hand, the Sales guys often ask her out, and the Accountants wire the home office for instructions.

180. I was a preferred stockholder; that means that while

other investors had to wait for a quarterly report to know the company was going down the chutes, they told me immediately.

181. The bad news is that Harry is becoming more and more schizophrenic. The good news is that at least I get two views of everything.

182. Harry says he slept like log last night; woke up in the fireplace.

183. Some guys are tried and found wanting, others are wanted and found trying.

184. He tries to act hardboiled, when he's really half-baked.

185. I don't mind a soft heart, but it's gone to his head.

186. Harry gave up all his vices once, but it didn't work out. Besides, he said it was the lousiest afternoon he ever spent.

187. Harry wishes he had saved something during the recession so he'd have a little to spend on prosperity.

188. The last time I spent an evening arguing with him, I told my wife I was sitting up with a thick friend.

189. Seeing Harry in that tux, people thought he was a waiter. One guy asked him, "Do you have frogs' legs?" Harry said, "No, these damn pants are just too tight."

190. The nurse made me take an eye test. She showed me a picture and I said, "That's the number eighteen." She said, "No, it's a photo of Harry talking to (name)!"

191. We'll go easy on Harry; he's had a tough day. Someone gave him a new boomerang and he's having trouble throwing the old one away.

192. Harry had laryngitis again last week. You can always tell. Everyone who works for him is smiling.

193. Harry burst into a doctor's office yelling, "Doc! Doc! What's wrong with me?" The doctor said, "Three things: you are overweight, far too dramatic, and you need glasses. The sign outside says I'm a veterinarian."

194. Someone asked me if Harry had a hearing problem. How would I know? When you're with Harry, about all you get to do is listen.

195. Sometimes I get hoarse just listening to him.

196. Harry has all the warmth and endearing charm of an alarm clock.

197. Harry has just written his autobiography. It's called, *Sex Takes a Holiday.*

198. If Moses had known Harry, I'm sure there would have been one more commandment.

199. We didn't know what to get you, Harry. After all, what do you get the man who has nothing?

200. Well, you can say this about Harry; he never let mediocrity go to his head.

201. Harry knew what the bosses wanted and he gave it to them: his resignation.

202. Harry is always saying, "Throw yourself into any project that you begin!" We're trying to get him to dig a well.

203. A man filled with the kind of love which surpasses all understanding: Self-Love!

204. Harry is suffering from a case of mistaken nonentity.

205. I was afraid I was going to be late. I got behind Harry at the confessional and there was a three-hour wait. It was the only time I ever saw a confession where the Priest requested an intermission.

IV. SEGUÉS AND TRANSITIONS

1. He makes you think of talent, competence, humility, and several other things he doesn't have.

2. I'll have to give you credit, Harry, you are a fantastic (title). You've always said that.

3. We shouldn't pick on him tonight. Earlier this very day his pet rat died in his arms.

4. You've been a Man of the Hour, a Minute Man, and now you're groping for the last few seconds.

5. That guy's got more bull than Merrill Lynch.

6. He won't drink coffee in the morning; says it keeps him awake all day.

7. In (number) years, he never quit a job; always got fired.

8. For years he believed that when he died the Trinity would become a Quartet.

9. Let's get on with this. We're all missing an "I Love Lucy" rerun.

10. He can take a dull and boring subject and somehow render it dry and lifeless.

11. You're not yourself tonight, Harry, and it's really quite an improvement.

12. (To a cigar smoker) Excuse me, are you by any chance an Egyptian Priest? No? Then why are you burning that mummy?

13. Oh, I could stand up here and be very funny I suppose, but why change the format of the evening?

14. Good old Harry, I wish there were a hundred of him. Trouble is there are a couple million of him.

15. He always remembered what Grandpa told him: before you fall in love with a pair of bright eyes, make sure it isn't just the sun shining through the back of her head.

16. If there were any more vice presidents around here, (the boss) would have to hold his staff meetings in two sittings.

17. An honest man; that's about as rare as an overworked lawyer.

18. That was quite a talk, Harry; some of the folks thought

you were a Chinese Philosopher. They said you were "On Too Long."

19. While folks were discussing why it couldn't be done, they were interrupted by Harry, who was doing it.

20. I regret to announce that for the second consecutive year, the (department name) Parade of the Virgins has been cancelled. Mary hurt her leg and Sarah won't march alone.

21. Harry puts a lot of fire into his talks. Now if we can just get him to put more of his talks into the fire. . .

22. People ask why our employees have to fly Tourist class. Easy; on modern airlines there's no such thing as Steerage.

23. Did you hear the juke box in the cafeteria today? If that's one of the Top Ten, you can imagine what the Bottom Ten must sound like?

24. Harry, that was a record never to be equaled again . . . provided the world ends at midnight.

25. The drug culture never caught on here. We can truthfully say there's no evidence that any of our executives took mind-expanding drugs.

26. We have a street in (city) named after Harry. It's called "One Way."

27. He was only whipped once in his life—and that was for telling the truth. It cured him forever.

28. When we make a movie about the company, we'll want you for the juvenile lead.

29. In (location) they just introduced a new deodorant that's so effective people don't know you're around. They call it "Vice President."

30. I asked him why he wasn't playing poker with the guys. He said, "Would you play with a guy who screws up the deal, can't remember the bets, talks incessantly,

and whines when he loses?'' I said no. He said, "Neither will they.''

31. Committee assignments around here are a lot like making love: long bouts of groping and sighing followed by a few seconds of total frenzy.

32. They call him the Chief Pharmacist of the New Product Group. Everything he produces is a drug on the market.

33. You can say what you will about the efficiency of government, but the U.S. runs an organization with a territory comprising several million square miles, 220 million people, and revenues of a billion dollars . . . all with just *one* Vice President.

34. Sorry I'm late. I was celebrating the tenth anniversary of my last promotion.

35. You've been a nice attentive audience . . . even if you did have your hearts set on seeing a juggler.

36. The Good News is that he gives us his best. The Bad News is what he calls his best.

37. That was very good! Harry always wanted to be a baggy pants comedian . . . so he could wear his own clothes.

38. (After speaker) Thank you, Harry, that was well read.

39. (After speaker) Thank you, Harry, that was good at both ends, if a little long in the middle.

40. (After speaker) Well done, Harry, those of us still awake salute you.

41. I'm not up here to deliver lines like Harry. For one thing, I've got too much judgment.

42. His life has been full of trials with an occasional conviction.

43. He must have a sixth sense. There's no sign of the other five.

44. He's spoken at many banquets and has never been hissed. It's hard to hiss and yawn at the same time.

45. He's not a loser. He just succumbs easily to overwhelming ability.

46. It takes courage to Roast the boss, (name), and I admire you for it. No judgment whatsoever, but lots of courage.

47. I'd like to remember you the way you were . . . employed.

48. That was a speech not to be forgotten . . . provided the world ends at midnight tonight.

49. Remember how you used to wonder what would happen to the little kid who took two hours to eat? Well, there he is.

50. Thank you very much, (name), I'm sure that little talk was a lot better than it sounded.

51. I'd like to explain the secret of the perfect speech to everyone on the dais. First, you need an attention-getting opener, then a rousing and thought-provoking close . . . then you get the two as closely together as possible.

52. I know now that Benchley meant when he wrote: "It's better to sit on your ass than to stand up and make one out of yourself."

53. You folks eat a little fast, don't you? I bowed my head to say grace, and when I looked up, they were serving dessert.

54. Now you know why sales resistance is a triumph of mind over patter.

55. None of these people know the "Exxon Rule of Public Speaking": If you don't strike oil after five minutes, stop boring.

56. Thank you. There was more claret than clarity in that little talk.

57. Thank you. You always seem to have a lot of words left over after you run out of ideas.

58. I find your talks very refreshing, (name)—I always feel better right after a nap.

59. Thank you. That little talk was up to your usual substandard.

60. Thank you. I think I would have enjoyed your talk more if I had a better seat. The one I had faced you.

61. You really have to know Harry to depreciate him.

62. Excellent job, (name), and very funny, too. For the first minute or so I couldn't believe it was you . . . then you proved it was.

63. Where I come from, we bury our dead. Here, you make them Roast Masters.

64. My friend (name) is, of course, English, and it is a pleasure to hear him read funny lines. They say the only way to make a middle-aged Englishman laugh is to tell him a joke when he's a small boy.

65. Thanks for that warm introduction. Beautifully, restrained, I might add.

66. Thank you, (name), that little talk ran the gamut from dull and uninteresting to thoroughly boring. It was a dead giveaway, though, when the audience went silent. I knew those must be the jokes.

67. Harry consented to this Roast because he is desperate to be recognized and remembered . . . by anybody under any circumstances.

68. Thank you for that resounding display of apathy.

69. He's about as memorable as Whistler's father.

70. Tonight Harry has been maligned, sneered at, and insulted; and rightly so.

71. If tonight you haven't heard a good word about Harry, it's only because we haven't let him speak yet.

72. Just wait till Harry gets up here. He'll have you open-mouthed with his stories. You won't be able to stop yawning.

73. I suppose you're all wondering why I called you here tonight.

74. But we're not here to discuss Harry's character in his absence; we're here to discuss Harry's absence of character.

75. Well, this has been fun while it lasted. Too bad it lasted longer than it was fun.

76. I think people laughed tonight just so you wouldn't be tempted to tell those jokes a second time.

77. Harry said to get up here, throw the script away, and just ad lib. He likes textual deviates.

78. When I came here tonight, I felt like a Daniel in a cage full of lions. Now that I've heard them all speak, I feel like a lion in a cage full of Daniels.

79. I don't mind picking on Harry. There's so much material there.

80. When we talked about Roasting Harry, someone said, "Just don't hurt his feelings." But all your friends and co-workers gathered around and said, "Harry doesn't have any feelings."

81. This isn't so much a company as it is a loose confederation of warring tribes.

82. Thank you for that little talk (name). I guess humor, like history, repeats itself.

83. His speaking that way reminds me of the Shakespearean actor who finally got his big chance to play Hamlet. Well, he had no stage presence, mumbled the few words he didn't forget, and generally made a fool of himself. The audience booed and started throwing things. He walked to the footlights and said, "Hey, don't blame me, I didn't write this crap!"

84. Thank you (name). It's very important for one good speaker to follow another. Last week I followed a very poor speaker, and right in the middle of my talk, they started booing him.

85. Thank you, (name), that little talk was like the horns on a Texan steer: a point here, a point there, and a lot of bull in between.

86. And then there's my friend (name): the only man I know who can finish a talk ten minutes before he stops speaking.

87. Just don't take any of this seriously Harry. Remember that if criticism really had the power to harm, the rat would have died out years ago.

88. And a word of advice for you, (name): a speech can be immortal without being eternal.

89. Do you know what it means when (name) says: "And in conclusion . . . ?" It means he is starting the second half of his speech.

90. I'm not up here to make a fool out of Harry. He'll do that himself later this evening.

91. I have an announcement: Harry will be checking our mail over the next several days, and we've been asked to cut down on big words.

92. The whole world's not against you, Harry. The people here tonight, maybe, but not the whole world.

93. Thank you for that glowing introduction and spotty round of applause. Let's see if I can convert your coolness into outright hostility.

94. Harry said I had the most responsible job in his department. Whatever goes wrong, I'm responsible.

95. Keep an eye on Harry, folks, and make sure he stays out here where we can see him. He sometimes gets bright ideas in dark corners.

96. Harry is a very humble man, and after you hear him you'll know why.

97. I haven't had this much fun since I worked nights in the stockyards.

98. Well Harry, I guess we couldn't have succeeded as we did without you . . . or at least without someone who had the same experience and skills.

99. Harry Gordon, a man whose reading and experiences have taken him to the heights and depths of business life. He's read all about the heights, and experienced most of the depths.

100. Now Harry, be sure to tell us if any of these stories bother you. Some folks who couldn't make it tonight have ordered a list.

101. I say, let's have more of Harry! Perhaps we can use him up.

102. Harry never thought of doing the things they do today. I guess that's why he never did them.

103. Did you hear that applause? It was like a caterpillar, walking across a shag rug, wearing slippers.

104. That little talk was vintage, Harry. I say vintage because of the influence the grape has had on Harry's career.

105. I didn't come here to honor Harry. I came here for revenge.

106. We have a lot of surprises for you tonight Harry, and we'd have even more if we had talent.

107. Harry, I've never forgotten you . . . though God knows I've tried.

108. Thank you. What that little speech lacked in wit and content, it certainly made up for in length.

109. Thank you, Harry. You have such a firm grasp of the obvious.

110. So far this evening has had all the charm and grace of a nuclear waste debate.

111. When (name) was asked to speak tonight, he first refused because he was afraid you'd all laugh at him. See,

(name)? I told you there was nothing to worry about. Not a single soul laughed.

112. (After waiter/waitress drops tray) Drinks are on him/her!

113. I have two kinds of speeches. There's my "Mother Hubbard," which covers everything from head to toe; and there's my "String Bikini," which covers only the most essential points.

114. Nicely done, nicely done! I still remember the first time I ever heard you speak. Every platitude hit home.

115. Now you know why this is called an auditorium. It's from the Latin root "Audio," meaning "I hear," and "Taurus," meaning "the bull."

116. What's eating him tonight? Well, whatever it is, it will get indigestion.

117. I don't know why it is, but every time I stand up to talk, my mind sits down.

118. As the Indian Chief said when he saw the mushroom cloud over New Mexico, "Wow! I wish I'd said that!"

119. Harry said to me earlier this evening, "Is this dense crowd here to do me honor?" I had to tell him, folks, "No Harry, they are not that dense."

120. Here's a note from the restaurant manager. He wants to remind you that tipping is forbidden. Here's another note from the waiters. They want to remind you that drink and sex are also forbidden, and that doesn't seem to bother us.

121. Are you listening, Harry? I have to be sure folks. He has the attention span of a mayfly.

122. Sorry I had to hurry you along (name), but we only had you penciled in for tonight.

123. That reminds me; when we told everyone that we were honoring Harry Gordon tonight, they all said the very same thing. Why?

124. What a polite audience! I was watching you all while he was speaking and you covered your mouths every time you yawned.

125. Good evening, ladies and gentlemen, I am Harry Gordon. If you'll kneel now, I'll give you my blessing.

126. I'm proud to be a friend of Harry's, and it's not easy being a man's only friend.

127. It's always difficult to follow another excellent speaker. Fortunately for you, (name), you don't have that problem tonight.

128. Your lines weren't all that bad. You just stood too close to the microphone and we could hear you.

129. Harry, there's nothing like a roast to find out who your friends were.

130. I think that talk was ghostwritten. He wrote it under an assumed mind.

131. Thank you for the comprehensive little talk. In one presentation you went from trespassing on our time to encroaching on eternity.

V. WRAP-UPS AND TOASTS

1. I call my (staff) *Surely, Goodness,* and *Mercy* because I think they're going to follow me all the days of my life.

2. Personnel announced today that the terminations would continue until morale improves.

3. He can take all this nonsense because he has the indifference to criticism which comes from success.

4. My idea of a great after-dinner speaker is someone who says, "Waiter, I'll take the check."

5. Harry, look at the crowd here tonight to help celebrate your retirement. As they say in show biz, "Give the people what they want and they'll turn out in droves."

6. Harry, when all is said and done, you've said a whole lot more than you've done.

7. You are my friends, for you have smiled with me, my help and hope in fair and stormy weather, I like you for the joys you've smiled with me, I love you for the griefs we've wept together. (Nixon Waterman)

8. I thank you for your welcome (which was cordial) and for your cordial (which was welcome).

9. Yes, we must ever be friends, and of all who offer you friendship, let me be ever the first, the truest, the nearest and dearest. (Longfellow).

10. She is my own, and I as rich in having such a jewel as twenty seas, if all their sands were pearls, the water nectar, and the rocks pure gold. (Shakespeare)

11. Here's to the merry old world, and the days be they bright or blue, here's to the fates, may they bring what they may, and the best of them all—here's to you.

12. To live in hearts we leave behind is not to die. (Campbell)

13. My friends ... I'm certainly not going to call you "Ladies and Gentlemen" after that little performance.

14. First of all, my compliments to the Roast organizers. How they ever thought they could bring this off without speakers or material will never cease to amaze me.

15. Here's to the joke, the good old joke, the joke that our fathers told; it is ready tonight and is jolly and bright as it was in the days of old.

16. Some of those lines were so touching, I thought it was a eulogy ... then I realized it was the speakers who were dying.

17. Sorry if I didn't seem to be paying attention tonight. I counted seven speakers on the dais ... and I was wondering when Snow White would show up.

18. I've had wonderful times in my life, but this wasn't one of them.

19. I know that even in years to come, I will think back on the memory of this evening, pour myself a cognac, sit in my easy chair in front of the fireplace, and upchuck.

20. Now that he's finally finished, we all know the meaning of the term comic relief.

21. Harry is a man of few words. The problem is, he keeps repeating them.

22. It's nice to be among friends . . . even if they are not mine.

23. I wasn't sure if you were honoring me or just draining off some old resentments.

24. The Hallingworth Toast: "Manufacturing is a very unsteady business, sometimes up and sometimes down, some few get rich, and thousands are ruined by it." To Manufacturing!

25. Well, are you all through? Were those your best shots? It was like being stoned to death with popcorn.

26. Harry, everybody wanted to get you some sort of gift, but we couldn't agree on what it would be. (Name) suggested a book on etiquette, but we ruled that out because it didn't have pictures. (Name) suggested sponsoring you for some sort of management course, but we all agreed it's a bit late for that. (Name) suggested a desk set of some sort, but your close friends tell us you're not to be trusted with leather. (Name) suggested an engraved gold watch, because you're not likely to last long enough anywhere to earn one on your own. And so, Harry, we settled on this (award).

27. A Roast is a rare medium . . . when it's well done.

28. It's been a fantastic and fun-filled evening . . . if you exclude everything that's happened up until now.

29. Thank you (name), you've been like a son to me: rude, surly, and ungrateful.

30. I had to cancel a dental appointment to be here tonight, and I'm sorry now I did.

31. A Toast: May you always be happy, and may your enemies know it.

32. A Toast: I wish you the four L's: Love, Laughter, Loyalty, and Length of Days.

33. A Toast: Health of body, peace of mind, an extra clean shirt, and a dollar.

34. A Toast: May we never crack a joke that shatters a reputation.

35. A Toast: Here's to you, old friend, may you live a thousand years; just to sort of cheer things in this vale of human tears; and may I live a thousand too—a thousand less a day; 'Cause I wouldn't care to be around and hear you'd passed away.

36. A Toast: May the Devil cut the toes of all your foes that you might know them by their limping.

37. You'll notice I've placed a sprig of mistletoe just under the tail of my coat.

38. Toast: To the Land we Love, and the Love we Land.

39. The audience, I noted, applauded your talk in three places: at the beginning . . . that was Faith! In the middle . . . when there was still Hope! And at the end . . . and that was pure Charity!

40. I just wish I had a dental appointment I could cancel. I need something to brighten my day.

41. Let me tell you a little more about why I'm leaving: First, my boss, (name), told me: "Harry, do something about your hair." So I had it styled a little bit. Then, he said, "Harry, work on that wardrobe a little bit." So I bought a few good suits. Finally, he said, "Harry, go take a few courses and develop a little more of a sales presence." So I went to Dale Carnegie and a couple of others. Then one day, I looked at myself in the mirror and I said, "Harry, you deserve a better job," . . . so I found one.

42. (Name), your talk was much better! You had a good

beginning and a strong, humorous close. It was only in the middle that you fell apart completely!

43. (Name), you had a fine beginning and an excellent close! We were all just wishing that they could have been closer together.

44. That the good die young will never be said of your jokes.

45. (Name), now I know what they mean when they say: "A fool and his microphone will soon be connected."

46. I came here tonight freely, with an open mind, without any sort of prejudice, willing to listen to what I know was ninety minutes of pure garbage.

47. A Toast: I wish you good health, long life, continued prosperity, and eventually, a measure of respectability.

48. Thank you for your support. I shall wear it always.

49. It's not fair: you guys had all night to make fools of yourselves and I only got a few minutes.

50. After a dinner, you usually have to listen to a long dull speech. Thanks to our hosts, tonight they broke that up into several shorter dull speeches.

51. They said to be humble, and I tried. I have never been so humiliated in my life.

52. It's not just anyone who gets the honor of being roasted. First, you have to be listed in the telephone book.

53. A toast to Harry. You have been rich and you have been broke; but, my friend, you will never be poor.

54. As the last speaker of the evening, I feel a little like Liz Taylor's latest husband: I know what you expect, but how to make it interesting?

55. He considers himself quite the wit. Well, I guess he's half right.

56. Just don't ever change, Harry. We'd like to forget you just the way you are.

57. It's such a treat to see you all in the audience tonight.

It means you are not talking behind my back . . . or worse yet, working late without supervision.

58. Well, as the firefly said when he backed into the power mower, "I am just delighted!"

59. So far, this evening has been one of the finest affairs I have ever slept through.

60. Harry, this is a handsome leather desk set which includes a ruler marked in millimeters. That's from all your friends who have learned never to give you an inch.

61. Harry, this gift was the unanimous choice of all the folks who have worked for you over the years. It's a book of etiquette. Don't be afraid of it Harry, it has lots of pictures.

62. Harry, we tried to think of something very serious and very appropriate; something to remember us by. We knew you'd never last long enough to earn a gold watch, so we said, "What the hell," and went out and bought you one. The back of this, Harry, will be engraved with your name, dates of service, and mention all of us here tonight who are proud to be your friends.

63. Well, at least the evening has had a happy ending. I for one, am glad it's over.

VI. FOR WOMEN ONLY

1. I remember her mother hanging out a sign that read: "Last Girl Before Freeway."

2. If you think she looks good tonight, you should see her in the morning when all the wrinkles are rested.

3. She's been banned from driving the state highway between 7:00 and 9:00 A.M. Apparently, the sun shining off her lip gloss has made her a road hazard.

4. The years have been kind to her; it's the weeks in between that caused all the trouble.

5. Another little-known fact: she was married once before but it didn't work out. They went to Jamaica on their honeymoon and she ran off with a steel band.

6. The last time she went into a beauty parlor, they tried to commit her.

7. When she says her food could melt in your mouth, she means you have to defrost it.

8. She used to be a school teacher but then she lost all her class.

9. Harriet is on the 140th day of a 14-day beauty plan.

10. Harriet said to me while shopping the other day, "Who *are* these people, Polly and Esther, and why do they make these terrible clothes."

11. I wonder how many orlons had to sacrifice their lives to make that dress she's wearing.

12. Harriet has a creed by which she lives: "If you can't go First Class, charge it."

13. Harriet does look good, after a fashion. After a couple of Old Fashioneds, she looks even better.

14. She bought some face cream advertised to take the wrinkles out of a prune. It didn't help her face much, but she's got the smoothest prunes in town.

15. Has anyone talked about Harriet's culinary skills? Her husband came home and found her crying because the dog had eaten a pie she had made for a special occasion. "Don't cry," her husband said, "I'll buy you another dog."

16. I won't accuse Harriet of poor housekeeping habits, but the other day she had a grease fire—in the sink.

17. And can she talk! I get hoarse just listening to her.

18. Harriet's husband says she does a great imitation of Teddy Roosevelt. She goes from store to store yelling, "Charge!"

19. Talk about conceit. When Harriet decided it was nearing time for marriage she said to me, "You know, a lot of men are going to be miserable when I get married." I said, "Really? How many are you going to marry?"

20. Sometimes Harriet, you're a sight for sore eyes; at other times, you're just a sight.

21. Harriet finally did it: she registered with a computer dating service. Last Friday night she had a date with Pac-Man.

22. She was one of the best secretaries we ever had (if you discount shorthand, typing, and filing).

23. Harriet decided to go on a diet. It was either that, or let out the living room.

24. Talk about being a prude? She willed her body to medical science with the stipulation that no one must ever peek.

25. She has suffered a lot for her beliefs . . . like, for example, the belief that she could still fit into a size five shoe.

26. Harriet spent the weekend running frozen leftovers through her microwave oven. Not so much to defrost them as to find out what they were.

27. Poor Harriet. She applied to one of those computer dating services and told them she wanted a male who was short and cuddly, who liked going out in formal attire, and who enjoyed winter sports, fishing, and swimming. They sent her a penguin.

28. I first met Harriet in 1981. That was her room number.

29. Harriet's husband says there's nothing to equal the experience of coming home from work, walking into the kitchen, and smelling the aroma of boiling water and roasting tinfoil.

30. Harriet's husband showed me a pocket handkerchief the other day. He said: "Look! They're starting to make tissues out of cloth!"

31. I asked Harriet how old she was. She said: "Somewhere between twenty-five and none-of-your-damn-business!"

32. Is she shrewd? She's so shrewd that the wool she pulls over your eyes is a polyester blend.

33. Here she is, direct from the senior prom at Castle Dracula: Harriet Gordon!

34. Here she is now, the Bank of America's Sweetheart: Harriet Gordon.

35. I once asked Harriet where she had learned so much about men. She said she went to night school.

36. It's hard to place Harriet politically: She drives an old car, dresses in current styles, and lives on future income.

37. I asked Harriet's husband, "Do you wake up grumpy in the morning?" He said, "No, I let her sleep."

38. Harriet's husband says she reminds him of an angel: always up in the air, harping about something.

39. The only problem Harriet has with the way she keeps house is that she can never tell when there's been a break-in.

40. Harriet injured herself the other night preparing dinner; got a bad case of frostbite.

41. Harriet said next vacation she was going to Yellowstone National Park. I said, "Be sure to see Old Faithful" and she said, "Oh, I'm bringing him with me."

42. Harriet thinks pedestrians belong in one of two categories: the quick or the dead.

43. Harriet shops like a bull: charges everything.

44. All Harriet's clothes are from Saks: flower sacks, grain sacks. . .

45. She found herself a combination psychoanalyst/hairdresser. First he shrinks her head, then he combs it out.

46. She was telling us about her social life. She said, "Fri-

day I went out with Lloyd, Saturday I went out with Milton, and Sunday I went out with Rover." I said, "Rover? He sounds like a dog!" She said, "You should have seen Lloyd and Milton."

47. I always give Harriet her way. She's got a perfect right. (Pause) She's got a pretty good left uppercut too!

48. Harriet was a heartbreaker. She told us about one chap who proposed; said he'd die if she turned him down. Well, she turned him down anyway and, sure enough, thirty years later he died.

49. Harriet's husband says she is entirely responsible for his financial success. Frankly, he said he felt challenged to see if he could earn an amount that she couldn't live beyond.

50. When Harriet came back from Paris, she was telling us about the social whirl. "I went out with this masseur," she began, but one of the girls interrupted. "Harriet," she said, "you mean a 'monsieur.' A 'masseur' is a guy who rubs his hands all over your body, pinches you, and grabs fistfuls of your flesh." Harriet said, "As I was saying, I went out with this masseur . . . "

51. She can be so damned logical! The first day here, the phone rang and I said, "Harriet, please answer that!" She said, "Why? It's always for you?"

52. Harriet has courage. She once told her dentist, "I want a tooth pulled and I want it done fast. No time for gas or Novocaine, just get it out and get it out fast!" The dentist said, "Okay, which tooth?" Harried nudged her husband and said, "Well dummy, open up and show him the tooth!"

53. Harriet went into Saks and told the clerk, "I want to try on that dress in the window." The clerk said, "If you must, but we have dressing rooms."

54. Harriet says she's going to marry a rich old man; doesn't plan to give up her youth, just pawn it.

55. She's a natural diplomat. She uses a pill to get rid of a headache, and a headache to get rid of a pill.

56. I suppose you've all heard the latest scandal? The local art museum unveiled a lifesize oil of Harriet . . . in the nude. Her husband was furious. Harriet said, "Don't worry, nothing is wrong, they must have done it from memory."

57. She selects her designer clothes so that she's seen in all her best places.

58. She exercised using one of those flesh-reducing rollers, morning, noon, and night for about six months . . . and it worked! You should see how thin that little roller is.

59. Harriet just got her driver's license. Her husband says she's driven for twenty years, and probably half-a-million miles, and this is the first time she's ever sat behind the wheel.

60. Every time I think of her, I get a lump in my wallet.

61. Harriet asked her husband what it would take to get him to go on a second honeymoon. He said, "A second wife."

62. Harriet wanted to name her new baby "Oscar." She said it was the best performance of her life.

63. She's quite the driver. There was the time that she called her husband about a problem with the car. She said, "I think there's water in the carburetor." "Where is the car now?" he asked. She said, "In the lake."

64. Harriet and I were meant for each other. She snores and I'm deaf.

65. A note from the old home town, Harriet. Billy Perkins says to say "hello." He asks if you remember when he used to walk you home every night? Well, he's still there . . . and he's still with the vice squad.

66. We looked forward to a little gourmet cookery when Harriet bought all those foreign cookbooks. Now she claims she can't get parts for the meals.

67. She reads "Dear Abby" and "Ann Landers" religiously. It's comforting to know that in this nuclear age, with the Russians looking over our shoulders, and the Middle East near boil, there is still someone whose highest priority is someone else's sex life.

68. Harriet and her husband agree on one thing; he thinks nothing is too good for her, and so does she.

69. Harriet's husband was in a minor auto accident last week, and told the judge it was Harriet's fault. She had fallen asleep in the back seat.

70. Harriet, I'd like to see you in 3-D. That's my room number.

71. Harriet says her credit cards were stolen, but she doesn't mind too much. So far the thief spends less than she does.

72. Harriet has to watch what she says to her husband. They were talking about vacations recently and she said, "Take me somewhere I've never been before." He walked her into the kitchen.

73. Harriet is so creative! I went over for dinner one night, and she reheated leftover TV dinners. She called them "reruns."

74. I would gladly raise my voice to support Harriet, but she won't let me raise my voice in her presence.

75. Harriet, you are that rare human being who refines our manners, challenges our intellects, and endangers our morals.

76. Harriet was thirty-five on her last birthday—the last birthday she admitted.

77. I've known Harriet for a long time. Years ago, in fact, when we were kids, we were the same age.

78. Harriet, when I get old enough to stop hating girls, you're the girl I'm going to stop hating first.

79. Her husband agreed to buy her a mink on one condition. That she promised to keep its cage clean.

VII. FOR THE HECKLERS

1. I could form an attachment for you; it would fit right over your mouth.

2. You can save face if you shut the lower half.

3. I can't imagine what we'd do without you; but we'd like to try.

4. Next time you buy a toupée, friend, order the one with brains in it.

5. Friend, we'd like to see you "on top of the world." As you know, that's a frozen wasteland to the left of the North Pole.

6. I didn't know the (name) Zoo granted parole.

7. You know, with an I.Q. like yours, you should have a low voice, too.

8. They say that if a man has an empty stomach, he won't rest until he fills it. Unfortunately for us, the same is not true of an empty head.

9. I won't engage in a battle of wits with you; I couldn't bring myself to attack an unarmed man.

10. He's good to his family, folks; he never goes home.

11. Have you ever considered brain surgery? In your case it would only be minor surgery.

Index